Fragmented Doors

L. C. Fothe

This book of poetry is dedicated
to my loving wife, Marsha
who made every word possible.

Table of Contents

Terpsichore

Muse of a thousand floating notes

Voices propelled to singing words of joy

With flutes sending winged sound heavenward

To tickle the ears of those so assembled

O Terpsichore, Terpsichore, grand muse of poetry,

Fill my mind with triumphant words,

Descriptions to thrill and excite the listeners gathered,

Let me take them to horizons never seen

Glories never felt,

Lands of tremendous wonder and ease:

Together with the songs of Melpomene and

The luxuriant voice of Calliope

We can once again cover the lonely world

With upliftment and happy excitement

About the wonders of human love, affection, dedication;

Give to me the gifts of poetic grace

Wherein journeys of the heart, even when put through trials,

End in triumph and victory through the telling

And freedom dancing to overwhelming emotion

Flailing itself wildly inside the body and mind.

Come, Terpsichore, to the shores of the Greek Isles once more

Let us dance with words to the lilting sounds of your flute!

What Have You Brought Me?

Thoughts or images dart back and forth
Across vast areas without measurement
Desperation drives a vehicle of soft cloth
Slowly over crevices of widening girth.
Where has gone my peace of mind
Amidst agonies of coming demise?

A protective sheet lies lazy across soft skin
Conforming itself to a new image of life
Wherein the journey dissolves itself glassine thin
Before turning toward a fresh brightening sun
Toward which I wish to run in my attempts to escape.

Suits of finely crafted stitches give thread-loops purpose
Binding together tenderness like gentle love,
Calm inside breath's exhale brings easy repose
Awaiting warm hands to soothe away troubled brows –
Brows I never thought would need caressing.

Calls across a distant divide clear my apathy,
Turn solace into sparkling excitement instead,
Wearing garments of former promises happily
Traveling far away into dreams of adventure,
Places I had wished to go but am no longer able.

A pause opens its welcoming arms once more

I close my eyes and then squeeze my slow begging heart

I can still slip away in travels of my mind where

Room service can step discreetly behind a dark door –

I can move forward in my newly formed armor

Into fantasies I feel free to explore,

Futures to be planned and pursued in theory

Forgetful of glaring realities to criticize

That which can and can no longer be done.

Still is my glee present and pumping strongest

Wanting to believe in a twist away from reality

In silence I pensively concentrate on where next to run

Close my eyes to enjoy a refreshed journey to elsewhere

Though temporary may be my stay of execution.

When the Birds Return

The oriole sits alone

Contemplating an emptiness inside –

Hollow gnawing of memories

Rumble through the orange breast

Not quite as vibrant as it once was –

The irresistible desire to hop from branch to branch,

The automatic response to chirp loudly in chorus,

A drive to follow and to lead others,

Mates to attract and impress with grand plumage –

Somehow it all seems impossibly irrelevant

As if what was clear in motivation lost its meaning.

Eyes look to every side

Knowing what seen things stand for

But not why.

Other orioles leave him at a distance

He is content with that –

He remembers.

At the feeder is where confusion reawakens –

There is a comfort being offered

Yet the necessary actions are absent

Sleep keeps taking him unbidden

Into a darker realm even in sunlight.

He rests on top of seed

Unable to grasp the meaning

Finally he flits heavily to the ground

Taller grass feels oddly comforting

Reminiscent of the birthing nest he grew up in

The air is growing cooler

The light is fading to dark gray

He cannot hear the other orioles nesting

There is no homing sound to follow

The tiredness says it is alright to rest

The solitude turns seemingly correct

Eyes spasm closed again and again

Until new wings carry him aloft.

Last Refuge

Talking to myself
    Something best done with pain
Remembering freedom's
    Gasping for clearer aisles of sight
        Down which to stroll in dreamy peace
Searching for cessation
    Pleading with tangible grimace
Feeling along walls for designs of escape
    Tremors of frustrated rage
        Hollow out the last refuge of sanity

Repetitive words
    Expel themselves in hope
Wanting response from emptiness
    Demanding help to come from myself
    To stop the incessant onslaught
Not knowing if life
    A concept lost in deep misery
Will return exuberance
    Releasing me back into the wild
    To heartily breathe free and smile

A Glance in the Window

The continued living

of a place that once was,

Tidy things

souvenirs from a fair,

Those I knew

move

speak familiarity,

Fur of my pets

still glides under fingers,

A warmth exists

behind fragile glass,

We are all there

where we are not,

Yet I feel the reality

of an ingrained past

Living and breathing

in scenes of truth

Where none

are in danger of

sickness or death,

Circumstances

of doing what we knew

how to do;

Half-awake

I cry my longing

for these things,

Missing so many

ways in which we once were,

A window

separates us,

Real and unreal –

I look inside

both when awake

and in dreams

But

On which side

of the window

am I?

Ease of Being

I jump high to feel delight

Butterflies flit in full color

Stoop down to discover the earth

Caterpillars head for their next leaves

I sit on grass to feel connected

Breezes wash by on their travels home

I put out my arms as thin wings

Hawks circle above in exemplary grace

Smiles are my face of glee

Clear are my eyes of seeing

Smooth is my breath of ease

Filled is my soul with satisfaction

Circle of the Lost

We have made our moves

Circled each other

to vie for notice –

to pretend we are things

we are not;

When we hold the glass of ourselves

up to the telltale light

there is always something lacking,

something not quite right,

making us less

than what matters to us most.

How absurd to fool each other

And ourselves

With perceived antidotes for insecurity;

Born in the cribs

cradles

playpens of home –

carried into the yards of

school and classrooms

where we are thrust into

competitions with others,

Forced to become equals
in completely different realms,
punished
for not living up to
potentials of someone else,
not acknowledged
for how our individuality
makes us best.

Far too many years follow
in confusion of causes
continuing to twist our personalities
needlessly –
erasing much of what
we could have and
should have been.
Sadness
Disappointment
Failure
Too late do we seem to learn
where our sorrows were born.

Floating in the Dark

Formless

Blacker than darkness itself

They hover and drift

Not caring if seen or not

Scouring for discards

Scavenging

Puddles of night

Flowing belligerently

In rooms of despair

Floating reminders

We are being watched

Only the changing of the clock

Says that I've slept

And a groggy mind

Believes it is functioning fine

Who wants to know

What is really being felt

Or what an aging mind thinks

If I say I am afraid

Youth says,

"That's how old people are"

As if I had become nothing more

Than a stale crust of bread

To be tossed to

Head-bobbing pigeons;

Yet it must be remembered

Nature abhors weakness

Attempts to destroy it

At every turn –

Only the very few

Can teach themselves

Compassion

Still tossed am I

Far into unwanted corners

To be watched

For what I will become.

Together

Fences require mending to maintain form,
Bridges need monitoring for integrity,
Boundaries are set to comprehend spaces,
Walls provide two directions of privacy;

I have walked along roads,
Reached gates at the corners of properties,
Gazed across areas of perpendicular alignment,
Wondered what existed beyond those horizons;

Voices call my name from familiar places
Letting me know I am still wanted,
I bend to show affection to my loving dog,
Tail-wags fan my face with joy;

New places, old places, offer personal charms,
Either will do when earnestly desiring escape,
I listen to the calling approach of sleek black ravens
Together we shall feast while yearning for home.

Turning Minds

The sound is eternally clawing for

Demands to be fervently met

By those who seek the meaning behind why

As if the answer could solve the anxious riddle

Of life and living, of death and dying or eternity.

Perhaps we could sit at a table to

Sip steaming cups of herbal tea

While waiting for a curtain of truth to arise

Revealing our deepest seated enigmas in nakedness

No longer disguised in ambiguous words of philosophy.

Once I had a kitten cuddled in my arms

Its clear eyes staring up at me in their marble-like clarity,

I felt the pure transference of love and trust reserved for

Very few acknowledged moments of exchange between

Entities whose being lives outside the area of measurement.

If maybe all of these moments could be joined to

Maintain a continuum of colossal realization

Then we could understand and blossom beyond

Our tiny finite grasp on knowing, seeing, believing

Where we came from, where we are and where we are going.

We Have Been

Suspended lines

Repeating patterns

Protest savagely

Demanding solutions

Resolutions

Within the confined spaces

Of my mind.

Symphonies played

Opening concertos

Carrying music

Warm purity

Solace

Across conjoined synapses

Within my brain.

Down passageways

Blind alleys

Purposely obscure

Begging for bearings

Confused

Unrecognizable

Marooned in desolation.

Our mission

Symphonies of joinings

Intertwined

Harmonies of understanding

Becoming

Instruments we were not

Hearing

What our single mind

Could not invent

Forming

The complete orchestral

Presentation

Of who we have been

In symbiosis of love

A Very Long Walk

Wandering over the same footpath

Leaves muddy ruts behind

I groan with disparaged sight

The way ahead is hidden

By thick undergrowth

The woods are heavy with silent danger.

Questions remain unanswered

I look around at sameness repeated

The friendship of nature has turned toxic

Yet must I place one foot in front of the other

While motion is still available to me

To what shall I pay attention?

A silence only contains my pleas

An anger permeates all thought

Reasons for trudging on evaporate.

No morning joy of sunrise

No world awakening exuberance

Forward has become stagnation

Overcast is a non-existent sky

A renewing rain of refreshment

Will not be passing this way again.

Stepping into oblivion

Takes more effort than imagined.

Calibration

The day was different than other days

Eyes of the doe paused to reminisce

A scent in the air reminded her of something bad

Stream water flowed, her reflection fragmented,

She bent gingerly to drink

Her two fawn crept out from the undergrowth

To join in the hunt for their daily sustenance

These were the grounds of the doe's home

Deep within the mountain forest safety

They stopped in frozen pose, listening for predators,

Quiet, and mother's reassuring glance, released the fawn

Simultaneously they bent to eat fallen leaves

She walked away to leave them far behind for now

To keep them safe so hunters could only track her scent

The fawn continued to munch as they watched her disappear

Into the woods hundreds of yards downstream

A startlingly loud report soared through the air

The fawn froze, studied, listened, then
        darted into deep green safety

Wondering if the doe would be returning that night

To nurse them to comfort.

They dozed and waited –

They dozed and waited –

They dozed and waited …

Bring Me Back

That which lies upon a bier only deserves fire
We have seen the remains of life abandoned
Gone is the accustomed animation
Withdrawn are the sounds of celebration
Quiet emptiness takes the place of that which went before
Signs of reawakening are irrationally sought
        (or maybe even feared)

Let us not speak of death dear brother
Let it be of strength and prowess
Planning and longing and accomplishment –
Lift a glass to drink the ale in toast to friendship
To walking the high roads in search of discovery
Where grand adventure awaits around the next corner.
Let us laugh and even cry together over shared memories
Sail on waters of great mystery,
Give each other hugs of welcome and comradery,
Let us sit in silent musing and contemplation
Of time slicing frivolously away and
Of tomorrows feeling assured to arrive.

The crackling of fire along dried logs
Brings me back to where I was.

Chances

Roll the dice in these games of chance

Watch the pips tumble to the top

Excitement boils in that instant

Disappointment can follow just as fast

Eyes seeing what they didn't want

Another result thrown in the pot of failure

She said her flowers couldn't bloom this year

Too much iron in the soft moist soil

Always something hidden running the show

We will count as many blinking stars as possible

Watch the moon for its tantalizing light

Until an eclipse absconds with our beloved moonlight

Another day of rolling the dice

Hoping the goodness we want will appear

We cannot help but play the game

Take the Tour

Thought and knowledge lie in looking at your hands

What they have held and what they have wrought

Are maintained in their own memories of the past –

The residence of your definitive self

A place of storage for that which was seen and

Experienced and remembered.

What will be touched next is up for grabs

As to whether it will have form and mass

Or will it be something to be imagined to be

Physical – identifiable through living filters?

Turn your hands one way or another

Palms up or down

See how they begin to look like hands

Of those who have gone before you –

Hands of memories

But hands that may or may not be yours

Anymore

A Place I Found

The eye of tomorrow opened slowly to the East
> Surreptitiously focusing on what it found waiting:
> A vision of another eye watching
> From within frozen crystals of shimmering light

Having wept true tears of heavy loss

In the distance tall towers with golden caps shone
> High above thick green canopies of fresh breathing life:
> Birds in flocks rose ceremoniously
> As they sang with unusually high intensity of joy

In tones of pure happiness of laughter

Tranquility eased away all apprehension
> Frozen tears were the artifacts of yesterday
> Held in stasis so as not to be forgotten –
> Freedom of safe exploration set my sight free

I lifted myself onto the breezes of sweet melody

Will there be returns of certainties
> When crying was never necessary
> Awakening holding excitement of promise
> In the longings to touch, to feel, to live

When I still had you to fly these melodies with me

There is One

There are times of love

Times when good feelings abound

Times when not all can be said

Times when sharing means love

I have felt a distant hand in mine

I have felt empathy as truth

I have felt warmth as I sleep

I have felt caring bigger than the world

No one knows the deepest needs

No one sees the depths within

No one touches the greatest memories

No one vanquishes looming doom

Except one.

Revolutions

Up the stairs and down the hall

Past open doors leaning askew

Sunlight glinting on broken glass

Flakes of peeling paint

Lie scattered across dark wooden floors

Climb the old worn ladder

Through the rough opening to the roof

Cooing pigeons flap their wings

Waiting for their hard kernels of corn

The sky is exhibiting a relapse

Of everything it has been before

The neighborhood has grown quiet

Since the last solitary visit

A severely weathered bench

Affords a place to sit and listen

Only memory can fill in the voices

Names no longer matter as to

Who is still here or who is not

Fragments drift in and out

Without linear form

Many things have deteriorated

Even disappeared altogether

A sigh to the silence is all that can be offered
Nothing is left to see
Of the personal structures
Erected a lifetime ago
No matter how close or distant
A naked emptiness is all that remains
However much there may have been
Elements that defined personality
Continually evaporate into undefined elements
To be taken back to their birth places
In the eternal passing breezes
The pigeons gather around
Their pink feet and bobbing heads
Still only offer cold eyes of want
Of more food from pockets and
Curiosity
Wondering if the circle of visiting
And leaving
Has come to its final
Revolution

Look Away

Attend the stumbling poetic word

Performing in presence of a victory ball

Small leaps to notice a thought

Call mourners together – let them learn

Do the sparkling threads of an empty bed

Strive to spike a meaning overlooked?

Curiosity won't let voyeurs look away

Eyes have become dry and numb

Poets fly on glorious wings of art

Gentle are the rains in open minds

A window stands open – unendowed

Ravens peer in for a lost friend

Color of Love

A flowing river of separate colors side by side

Intertwine themselves with sinewy undulations

To invite followers to come join in the journey

Toward freedom in being exactly what they were meant to be

Jump in as one gloriously bright stream next to others

Trade and swap tonalities from bright to subdued

Meld in the touch of becoming fully whole

Feel true emotion within the life of a certain color

Taste flavors of who and what you have been when floating

An ease carries all along in peaceful unison

Together melding – intermingling without staining

Flowers pull up their roots to join the liquid parade

Where flows this river no one cares

Separate togetherness is its own destination

Tell Me a Story

Tell me a story in lines of pictures
    That jump up in my mind,
Let me follow the movement and thoughts
    Of someone else's view of the world,
Fly – fly into darkness with danger
    In hot pursuit to come out the other side
In light to vanquish the foe hard-fought
    And to walk away to heal personal wounds;

Show me lands to which I have never been,
    Rooms in buildings with new views and aromas,
Let me meet people with wonderful tales to tell,
    Feel romance for places covered in night air;
Travel on tram cars, street cars, rail cars,
    Take in the broad horizons streaking by,
Follow solid justification with noble goals in mind
    Resolve mysterious enigmas with the mind;

Temporary feelings of being a different person,
    Times of living an unknown life,
I will absorb every moment of escapism,
    I wish to make a new story my own.

The Hill

A cold cold winter gathers about me

Warmth has retreated in hibernation

Along with my friends

Shivering by myself is second nature

My comfort is a blanket around my shoulders

Grannies in rockers come to mind

How far ahead will this snow path reach?

I would love to sled once again

All is not as white as it seems

Interludes of pain and agony arise

Spike balls thrown with force

I am the one who cannot run

I hear buzzing of fluorescent signs

Smell leftover essence of beer

Then cry for companionship

The top of this hill is where we come

Many others have preceded me

Look down at its end

The slide is coming

Not the sled I had hoped for

Cold cold is the winter gathering about me

Drifting

Release the mooring rope from the dock,

Let's drift and rock out into the open lake

Distant greenery on the far shore defines us,

It points to the sky containing us.

Tiny waves make their lapping sound against the hull,

Fish jump and disappear again into their murky home

We are here to observe, not disturb,

We are filled with the awe of natural existence,

Listen carefully to hear the passing of the breeze

Knowing it is only really here because we are;

Quietude pulls us gently into ourselves

The Mackerel King smiles beneath our bow

Let us simply drift here for a while

Where we will never be again

Breathe in deeply the daylight of divine passing.

Etcetera

Sometimes I can be found staring at the wall –

It is far better than staring into a mirror –

Scenes blink and change without instruction

Silver-haired ladies bend to say you have a cute dog

The days were once long

Now it seems to be the nights

Coffee was for caffeine

Before it became entertainment

I wait to watch a novel being written

About a man with indigo skin chasing snakes

Far into a jungle realm until he finds quicksand –

Snakes can be tricky like that –

If I tried to capture the scene with a camera

A blank painted sheetrock wall is all that would show

Not meant to be

He just sits and stares

Is there something wrong with him?

This is the Café of open dreams

Others come to forget where they are

Oh look! Goats climbing rocks

Sheep grazing comfortably

Feel their soft wool under eager fingers

Running can be exciting
When the destination is nowhere
But stop to watch the ants
Diligently gathering and building
That which can be so easily destroyed
Intriguing
I walk without care
Through the silence of a night
Breathing in the fullness of myself
Alone
Feeling somehow refreshed
Free of the infection of others
They see a man sitting by himself
At a table with his pen, paper
And cold coffee
My screen goes blank
My eyesight blurs
It was after all
Just a wall

Everywhere Everyday

On park benches they can be found

Feeding eagerly waiting pigeons and sparrows

Old men and old women

Lost in a world that no longer finds them valid

Discarded human beings told to go home

And stay there

Their children work their own families

In other parts of the world

Younger business associates have no time

Friendships were frail like thin-shelled eggs

Evaporating in the sun

At least it is known

Exactly what the birds like and expect

Their greetings and happiness are genuine

They bring temporary smiles

Along with mumbled words of affection

It is enough to have at least this in a downturned life

Before the trip back to an empty house begins

Searching for Lost Lives

I am a derelict in a suit of skin

No plans for an inoperable forward gear

Futures and pasts are blending like melting ice

Visions flow in or out in fuzzy distortions

As if trying to be focused with the wheel of binoculars

I wander dejectedly through echoing rooms

Of a dirty abandoned orphanage

The floors are covered in fallen debris

Walls have an unhealthy feeling

Despite bright spots of childish colors remaining

Where did all the children go when care stopped?

They could not have been turned off like electricity.

Wandering from one dark room to the next

I hear phantom voices, laughter, crying, memories

Feel twisting pitiful fears still attached to this place

Molding coloring books next to disintegrating crayons

Story books that will never open again

Cold empty bedframes rusting in place

Chairs no one would ever want to sit on

A huge dining hall too eerily silent

Bathroom facilities look terribly odd when abandoned
Electrical panels and conduits ripped apart
Window air-conditioners strewn on the floor
Copper torn away needed someplace else
A deteriorating nakedness permeates it all

I came to be here for a reason – a recognition
It's not the same as it once was – unrecognizable
The air is too dead – too still – I must escape
Down hall after hall I rush in a sudden panic
The sun has set on the other side of these walls

Darkness of a palpable variety leaves me trapped
I can no longer see to move
Please, I don't want to stay here
I can't find the exit
Where is outside?
What is outside?

Who am I anymore?

That Which is Inside

I use my mind to find the avenues
Flowing on their own in myriad directions
To bring gifts of the bread of knowledge –
The bread of understanding –
To the darker parts of my impoverished brain;

It is a monochrome journey of spiraling trails
Where questioning horses seek me out for love,
Anxiousness is in their large searching eyes,
Needing to feel non-aggressive trust
To help them find their way back home

Let us move in unison toward an imperative,
Find the floundering core of intention,
Seek the reason of separate awareness;
In a world of concrete and false pride,
To rediscover the touch of the lost ones.

When I break down with sadness on the journey,
Warmth from the travelers' hides surrounds me –
Comforts me – stays with me till the danger passes
And we move on together with renewed confidence
That fear will not cripple us from finding genuine solace.
A velvety blue coolness suddenly surrounds us

We can see more clearly than ever before
As we share in the basket of universal bread
A tent has beckoned and allowed entrance
Together we all step inside without being afraid

A veil of confusion lifts from our eyes
A different sight allows us a true view of each other;
We have lain ourselves down in shared love
Our new eyes have closed in the peace of knowing
Tenderness has touched and healed us this day

Silent Watch

I cry my tiger tears
  Hot, rolling down my cheeks
Blurred are my gardens
  Sad, watching me with angst

Salamanders on my left
Lizards on my right
Pause on bowing leaves
To mourn with me
In orange daisies
Bringing memories of youth
Mother and Grandmother
Collecting Mother's Day flowers
Wafting deliciousness of gardenias

I wait for my dog's bark
  Distant, racing home for love
Silent stillness comes
  Instead, breaking my heart more

Streets to wander
Emptier than ever
Nowhere awaits my coming

Lost in my own fields of being

Listening to my breathing

No one seeks me out

Another day like today

Tears become useless

Listening is futile

Waiting is a fool's game

Is anyone thinking of me?

Dream People

Dream people walk next to me

I never see their faces

But friends they seem to be

I am comfortable

Sometimes male

Sometimes female

Mostly silent while I talk

We always have a destination

Dangerous strangers

Want to find us

Chase us

Hurt us

We run

We hide successfully

Until dream friends

Disappear

But that too feels right

I sneak away

I escape

At least enough

To find my way home

By waking up

Knowing we will travel

Together another night

Abstraction

I held in my hands small plastic frames

With moving pictures inside

They were supposed to represent

Where I have been, where I am now,

Where I am going

Except

I didn't recognize any of it

A face stared out at me

Waiting for me to activate it

I don't know who it was

The raw flow had no metaphor

It couldn't be made pretty

Or melodic

There was no spigot for me to turn it

On or off

Involuntary screaming, begging,

Cursing are the insane babblings

In a world unattached

Unhinged

Suddenly I saw

Another person in front of me

She had a dirty white bow

In her disheveled hair

As she leaned on folded arms

On the top of a fence while

She sobbed

In another time

Another form

Misery aimed to the right

Stare fixed on an endless distance

I felt empathy without compassion

I looked back down at the framed pictures

They were static

Lifeless

No kisses or hugs

No remembered security

Just stale

Mementos

On someone else's piano

Understanding

Wind ran wildly through my clothing

Rain mercilessly pelted my face

I stood perfectly still

Pondering the worth of a sword in a storm

Across the valley were lighted tents

Allies or enemies? I did not know

Dark clouds moved

The moon was uncovered

Shimmering silver drops slowed

Muffled sounds of living

Drifted over the distance

Humans neither friend nor foe

Demonstrating

Simply life being lived

In voices of their own

I am an outsider needing warmth

A chill of feeling deserted runs deep

Yet in self-awareness lies peace

A meditation on emptiness

My voice cries in unison with the universe

The sense of a dark cave surrounds me

As if I had risen to a reminder of life

Having to be lived

Apart

In solitude

Thinking Slow Thoughts

The world lies in trees upon the lawn
> Dusty moons bring morning fog

An old man's shaking hands betray
> The rock-hard mind of his loving heart

Deeper looks to see higher meanings
> Cats over fences, dogs in pursuit

The shadows of sad mourning trees
> Kiss the ground like keepers of time

Fleeting moments of lasting glory
> Illusions within a thirsty mind

Fading sight of one living long
> Cannot see the missing pieces

Men in blackened corners appear
> Distant howling of bodyless dogs

Desires to write lists for useless holidays
> A last forgotten thing to do

Night closes eyes of a slumbering town
> Quiet in the blessing of sleep

One sits at an open window
> Waiting for the vendor of life to come

Remembered Things

At any given moment over coffee or tea

A relaxed wandering mind goes exploring

Digging deep into the treasure chest of goodies

Saved for times just as simple as these

Where scenes of swift remembrance paint anew

Feelings, sounds, aromas, vibrations

Of smiles amidst sincerest words of love

Or the sense of absorbing surreal landscapes within

And without.

"Where have you gone?" is what the nightingale sings

Knowing your heart is on a flight of its own

Out to find the best parts of being yourself

Alive in private spaces of recall and glory

With saturated vibrancy in a touch of warmth

From having known another found in your seeking

With whom sensations could never be repeated

Learned meanings of what affection should be

Desire, romance, happiness, fulfillment

Being only words falling short of what the soul absorbs

While pure smiles now come to your face unbidden

And

Another cup would be nice

Through the Keyhole

It was through a keyhole I slipped

To the other secret side where

I wished to be.

Clamorous vibrations drew me

As metal filings to a magnet

I approached heavy thrumming patterns

Resounding in continual beating of drums

The pounding ached in my soul

I swayed

I writhed

Arching my back in sensual surrender

Eyes fixed on a past of monolithic stone

The sky cracked open like an ugly gash

Ten thousand dark birds of prey descended

And spread themselves across every direction

Seeking what they came to feast upon

The Just cried with joy

The Corrupt ran in sweat

Horses brayed to the howling of hounds

Black figures folded out of dark corners

And tried to sneak away

Chaos clenched its fist of control

Everything paled and bowed in fear
Even those who thought themselves prepared
Fell to the ground in awe
Marble and stone tombs crumbled
The ground split open in violent upheaval
Erected edifices collapsed into dust
Dams burst to gush forth churning waters to
Sweep away the needless and the worthless
Hour upon hour the din continued
Amidst howling, screaming, bawling, begging
Until time lost its meaning and then became
No time at all
I drew in a breath at the sound of approaching
Silence
Quiet of that magnitude was painful
At a great distance a golden light glowed
As it moved slowly over the decimated land
Like a collector mining for gold
Searching the thoughts of existence
To the left, to the right
Sweeping like a golden broom
My eyes remained fixated on the motion
As my mind began to grasp its own condition
I felt myself begin to cry
A shaft of white

Reignited my doorway
I slipped back through the keyhole
Back to the side from which I had come
The re-emergence washed incessant sound
Over me until the pain made me grimace
I went seeking truth and
Found so much more
I think I will stay where I am for a while

Clouds of Purity

I am washing the fences with the purest of water

So I can more clearly see through the cracks

Memories of Chinese New Year celebrations

Reverberate in my mind

Colors in motion, swirling to a natural rhythm

Oversized masks of toothy smiles

Make the children run screaming

I am in a place where I work and smile

And smile and work

And craft my place the way I like

I see the dragon making its snaking way toward me

Turning its head to and fro

Preparing to rear back to celebrate in firing smoke

And flame

Firecrackers crackle and pop explosively in long lines

Out with bad luck and in with new

Colorful streamers with over-sized confetti

Waft and float through the air

I am amazed at feeling giddy inside

The dragon smoke covers me, engulfs me,

Carries me away to float on clouds

Wherein I see nothing but pure cleanness

In every peaceful direction

I embrace the mane of the dragon momentarily

Then good fortune moves away

My cloud dissipates into reality

I see the dragon spasm until it comes apart

I tumble to the hard unforgiving ground

Awaken

To a sudden forgotten misery

Without purity

Or pity

Subterfuge

Time soaks up my capacity for waiting
Doors that were once open
Are now all closed
Welcome mats lie abandoned

I hear her voice calling to me
Her name is one I should know
Three hundred sixty degree turn finds nothing
I must have been mistaken

Could the pictures that fell off the wall
Into a broken heap on the floor
Represent a simple vibratory accident or
Be the sign of something more insidious?

Where have gone the days of good surprise –
The gold mines of happy discovery?
When did dread and fear creep in –
As darkness tries to cover daylight?

I have read words filled with promise
I have been soothed by distracting comforts
It must be a duty of the mind
To keep me sane through subterfuge …
… yet still I believe …

Above

There is something soothing about the sound

Of sparrows chattering hidden under eves

You see them peeking out to look down at you

Then dart away quicker than your eyes can follow

Babies in the nest is what you hear now

Making their little peeping sounds

For food to be given and warmth to be returned

The parent flies back with something in its beak

Squeezes back into the opening

And the crying of baby birds goes quiet

It is moments of notice like these –

Remembering that other parts of life exist –

Being equal or even above

The petty worries that want to control

Our miniscule lives

It is moments like these that remind us

We are not alone

A Way Away

Coalesced in my hand

I see a world on fire

A house burning unnoticed

A destruction unplanned

Certified to a degree

I have the words to recall

A salvation coming uncluttered

A construction for me

Her hand flicked away dust

Words remained empty

Plants on the ledge waiting

Plastic flowers need no water

I wish to take back

Cruel words stated

Forgive my uncouth side

Forgive my careless lips

Redesigned by my iris

I seek a freeze rescinded

A youth climbing unburdened

A benediction from crisis

Humans

I know not where to go to regain the rebel in me
I have read your stories stretched across the backs
Of barefoot wanderers in the ancient cities. They
Attest to the ruination of thought by selfish pursuits
That leave behind trails of callous indignation.

All the other voices need to rise up to stop
Those of the "me – me – only me" who pour
Their opinions like wet concrete over grass
Attempting to blot out the art of simultaneous creation

My hands grow stiff, my lips grow cold
The collapse of Greece and Rome come to mind
I need the swirling beauty on canvas and
The myriad outpourings of monumental printed words
The melodic music of strings and united voices
Singing to the continued evolutionary growth of us all
Humans with humans about humans for humans
The same

Sludge

He crawled through the sludge of a mindless game
Wherein desperate faces popped in and out of focus
In order to scream their attention-getting refrains
Designed for induced confusions to be sheepishly followed.

He knew there must have been an obvious formula
Shortened wings needed to learn a new way of flying
Self-spoken words required situational adjustment
Yet his mind continued to crawl through unwanted places –

Scenes with strangers roaming about with objectives
Connotations of dreams bringing pleasureful relief proved false
Confusion remained in play instead.

He wanted violet flowers sprouting from purple earth
They smiled and tried to hand him fistfuls of plain dirt
Incessant dripping in the background caught his attention

When he turned the birdbath was already filling with mud
The time of refreshed renewal had obviously passed
His wings could no longer be cleaned and preened
The mindless game had returned for him to crawl
    Through more sludge.

Rebirth

Sandalwood incense burned

Eyes closed to sitar strums

Relaxed meditational drifts

The physical world withdrew

The sky was sought

Higher than Earth

A slide into Nothingness

Demons converged

Jealous

Tempted

The unsuspecting

With chains of false belief

Dragged the essence

Screaming

Boundaries lifted

Suffering presented

Shown without relief

Ignored

No fear felt

Not disturbed

Kept seeking the Infinite

The Unknowable

Only Light flared

Demons fled

Silence of Nothingness

Descended

Sandalwood sizzled

Breathing produced peace

The All of Nothing was born

Which?

Into a one-armed space I crawl

Waiting

Watching

Listening

A chiming sounds in the distance

Lonely carrots cry from within the earth

Events revolve on a feeling

Hidden

Cringing

Wary

A world of darkness approaches

Streets emit silence of empty design

The underside of a belly is strange to look upon

    A different world begging to be understood

        Frightening in its vulnerable presentation

            Like the desire to watch an accident in slow motion

            Curiosity can only drag us so far

        Until we can no longer be sure

        Of exactly who is dragging whom

"]

From where I hide the world is large

Towering

Overwhelming

Threatening

Another chiming in the distance

Is it a warning – or salvation?

I stay in my hidden safety

Wanting

Hoping

Praying

I have lost my discernment

For what is a pleasant call for me

From the Sky

Too many days they said
Go catch the rain
On the roof with a bucket
We ran joyfully from side to side
Ping. Ting. Bloick. We got Splashed
Our hair hung in clumps and we laughed
Few tiny drops broke free
We held out strong
With the bucket heavy in our arms
We never questioned why we did it
We were proud of our vast talents together
Building useless memories
Out of falling water from the sky

In the Dark

It was once, and then long ago,
Songs were sung to love

To joy

To heartbreak

To the future

Waiting for us all down the line;

Tears were shed when she left

Drafts through the door

From departing

Empty rings

Broken promises

Dim forecasts in the void

The air to breathe changed quality

Light was too bright

To watch

To wait

To stand

A next meal taken alone

Unwanted silence, a grandfather clock

Closing doors

Empty chairs
Abandoned roses
Cold bed for the restless

Floods of thoughts, fresh pain rising
From memory
From mistakes
From regret
Far out of reach to repair

No page to turn, the book was gone
The story had expired
No fanfare
No epitaph
No sequel
Only a vacant heart in the dark

The Pond Has Grown

So many faces have disappeared

Absorbed into the void of the past

Did I love them then?

Do I love them now?

The wheel spins but the ball doesn't land

The "now" swims in its own cold waters

Tomorrow replaces today – but just barely

Is there still love left to feel?

Is there still love left to give?

The water grows deep – I struggle not to drown

To Whom It May Concern

To whom is that man in the corner speaking
    as he faces the wall?
Clearly he cannot be right in the head to be engaged
    in such strange behavior.
Shoulder shrug. Who knows? Who cares? Just so long
    as the conversation is interesting.
The animation is sufficiently profuse so as to appear
    Very convincing to any passersby.
The words, however, have become impossible to hear
    Or decipher.
Then again, to listen in would be eavesdropping and that
    Is considered to be plain rude.
The back of his head and demeanor look familiar. I believe
    it is my father –
But he has been gone four years now. I should know –
    I watched him die.
Yet, there he apparently is, speaking to someone or
    something I cannot see.
Maybe it is not meant for my eyes and ears – or maybe
    I am the delusional one.

I Waited

Oh God! I saw them burning and bursting

As they came up from white marble slabs

Only disembodied heads, close to the ground

Wavering side to side

Their hair was disheveled – almost wispy

Their faces did not look right

A vindictive glare was in their eyes

Why were they lifting toward me?

What did they want? What did it mean?

I was afraid

I knew I did not want to reach in and save them

Compassion ran like a deer into the woods;

The reeling spinning of time disappeared

Beneath a churning of white smoke

Complex spikes shot up into the air as they

Whizzed past my head, laughing as they went

The goings-on beneath, below, and in front of me

Stayed hidden within the continually thickening smoke

I felt no flame or fire, heat was never even there

I could hear them moving, approaching, travelling –

But I could not tell where as my skin crawled;

Why was I here? (Wherever here was) Why could I not run?

Why didn't I run?

I shouted into my hands for some sort of help

I heard the word "obsession"

Cr y p tic

Suddenly the smoke cleared

The faces had turned the other way and

Remained still

Waiting

As if someone had flipped a switch;

I too watched and waited

For what or whom I do not know –

It did seem like a time of choosing;

Someone was standing next to me

I felt I knew him though I did not turn to look

He did not speak, only stood motionless

A companion, possibly a friend;

I would say I looked forward but

There was absolutely nothing beyond the heads

A dread of emptiness filled my fiber

I could almost hear a laughter at my fear

A misty fog approached and was growing

As it surrounded my companion and me

I felt as if I was suddenly standing in a cloud

Nothing but whiteness all around

Heavy tiredness came over me – limbs non-existent

I wanted to call out names I knew

But there was no voice to be found

I was alone

Instantly vast water appeared without sky

The white slabs lay across it like stepping stones

Then the heads reappeared, each to its own stone

Their countenance was no longer angry or vengeful

Yet I still knew not what I was being shown

The fog reappeared

I drifted into the cloud

I was no longer afraid

My companion was again next to me

In my head I clearly heard

The rest is not for you to know

Last Day

There's a last day coming
It's peeking around the bend
Do I wave it on in?
Unafraid?
Do I pretend not to see?
Turn away?
So many thoughts race through
Singular lack of understanding
What is the meaning of leaving?
Where will I go?
How much of me goes with me?
I have seen death
It looks very empty to me
Birds fall to the ground
We think nothing much of it
Why should it be any different
For me?

Warm Love

There is no time for the fleeing blind

They run furiously on their own

Windows flash by as shopkeepers watch

Safe behind their stiff glass barriers

Shoppers clutch their packages tighter

Grandmothers rock with a knowing wink

Strong wind swings the wooden signs

Careful gardeners clip overgrown hedges

Who ever knows who runs from what

When running has been honed to state of the art

A swift breeze passes from those who run unnoticed

Until suddenly someone has the sensitivity to know

Their hand reaches out to clutch another

To bring safety and security to the confused one

Scattered running ceases amid tears of gentle gratitude

The feeling of warm love overcomes all else

Barons

I took a thought
Threw it across the room
A bouquet of plums exploded
Barons strut tall in the road
We clapped to thunderous drums
Fancy heads bowed and moved on
Colors spun in pinwheel frenzy
I could not help but stare
She was next to me
Wry smile to posed lips
She leaned on my shoulder
Doubts flew empty into air
A new bouquet bloomed
Filled the room with petals
Sweetest scent
Velvety softness
I breathed deep
Absorbed tender thought
The barons bowed down
To fresh living royalty

Beyond

Say that you can sing to the night time sky
Send those melodies to the thirsting heavens
Words of deep caring with personal love
To each and every point of glistening starlight
And to the moon glow of millions of nights
All for the sake of divine heart's announcement
Of your existence, your indestructible spirit,
Your knowing of the travelling to the beyond
Where the curtain is opened and drawn away
To show the birthplace of those lights in the sky
But
In the meantime
Use the keys you possess and
Sing your beautiful songs to the night time sky

One Rain

Torrential rain came to ease my mind
Though I did not hear a sound
Bird bath splashing amid giggles of glee
Took control of the transposing scene
Windows flew open
Flower pots shook with excitement
Fair ladies and mannered gentlemen
Smiled gaily from behind sheer curtains
A world of understanding was awakening
True horns of joy announced the arrival
Clean breeze caressed the freshly washed earth
Wild livestock shook their heads in agreement
 I heard the hooves coming for me
Horses' heads tossed me happily onto their backs
We rode, we rode, we rode in jubilation
Fancier skies of clarity shone across muscular trees
Meadows and fields thickened their green embraces
Doves nested and rabbits rolled in succulent clover
A lone drop fell from above and rolled down my cheek
I felt as if we had all come home

Step Outside

Inside a transparent bubble we ride

Wide-eyed we stare in every direction

Together we hold hands for emotional reality

Sharing the hidden beating of our hearts;

Nothing is as we once thought it was

Smooth became rough, rough became careless,

Too much more was found to be insignificant,

We grimace at realizations of cold truth;

Ah but then there are the intangibles-

The beauty, the mythic, the imaginative –

They swirl before us like prismatic bubbles of soap

They float on drafts of clear happiness

Bobbing and dancing in coordinated chorus

Begging for our delight and discovery

As they are drawn to the absolute miracle

Of an indestructible bond of hands being held;

We receive their gifts of inspiration

Of insight

Of creativity

Propelling us toward gateways of appreciation

We can share with an otherwise colorless existence

Together we can fill our bubble with awesome color

Open windows and doors to step outside

Away from our isolation

Into the sounds of finely textured love

Where we say we can remember how to smile

How to dream

How to find ourselves

Written to Remember

At his desk is where he sat

Filtered sunlight splashed innocently across its surface,

Blank paper in its virginal whiteness

Lie before him,

A pen motionless between slack fingers:

He leaned his head on an upturned palm

And wondered what tomorrow may bring;

The tweeting of a Nashville warbler beneath the window

Drew him into another world of life

Transporting his attention instantaneously

Far beyond the reaches of worry and despair

His ears followed the intonations as he wished he knew

Exactly what those high-pitched notes meant –

What was so clear to others of its kind?

Rhythmically repetitive in a happy way

Embers of creativity awoke to their calling;

In a moment of clarity the reason for leaving words

In forms for others to follow

Became the shared language of experience –

Expressions of impressions travelling

Across the senses to be interpreted –

To feed on discovered pathways of living

Absorbing the feelings, the sounds of motion

In the calling of birds

In the swelling of their breasts

In the taking to quick flight

And the episode continues in the brain

He imagined the dance and prance of the warbler

Across thin branches until it flitted away

His pen came to the paper to spread words –

Words to spread visuals across the mind

For feelings of timeless 'here and nows'

Stories of mysteries fraught with meaning

Places seldom seen with physical eyes

Emotions sparked to tenderness

Songs to be sung

Flights of freedom to be taken

Where escape is the reality of being

And sharing is the penultimate act of the living

Written

Stored

Remembered

Going Somewhere?

Feel your way through dense fog

Safety and security run away

Fear jumps into your throat

Imagination turns on itself

Orientation becomes reality of the past

Complete aloneness presides

You walk within an earthbound cloud

Slowly slowly ever so slowly

Mists move past your vision

To move or not to move

Which will it be?

Wait for something to come for you

Or go searching for it yourself?

You expect the evils of a child

Or evils out of the news

If a hand were to touch you

You would scream

A dog races past in terror

Escaping

In out and through the fog in front of you

Chills crawl up your skin

You didn't even hear it coming

Worse yet

What lies waiting in the fog ahead?

You won't hear it coming either

＊＊＊

Find Truths Deeper Within

A little room we accept as a closet

is indeed a total room of its own

holding facets of the whole personality,

no one notices

it is a person on display –

Colors, shapes, self-appealing tastes,

every mood can be found there

to tell tales of who they are

who they were-

told better than volumes of written description:

Parties, celebrations, weddings, family gatherings,

seductive settings, feel-good days, sadness,

playful events, work time necessities, religious duties,

Funerals –

One must only look to the meanings

of those things to be found within

deep inside the reasons behind the choices,

the desired aura to be projected

at a given moment in time,

the memories made for the mind –

Inanimate objects given life sparks

of where, when, and why –

so much more than the dull eye perceives,

all reside within this overlooked storage vault

held secretly in the privacy of a personal closet.

60 Seconds to Nowhere

Organizing thought out of chaotic ramblings
Produces pictures of immense proportion
But they become glimpses of madness
That bubbles beneath the surface of insanity
As pretense to intelligence of an alien nature.

Outside worlds, internal universes thrive
On building personas subject to crumbling
Where questions of *who am I* stagger from
Weights and shackles of expectation
Leaving their helplessly lost victims adrift.

Stand as an ibis in the shallowness of calm waters
Wait for something delectable to drift nearby
When suddenly upheaval from below throws
Every planned motion into extreme upset
Changing the natural order of learned behavior.

When the water calms, only scraps remain,
Unrecognizable as to being what once was –
Abandoned perceptions float away like smoke
Walking turns reptilian in halted glimpses of distrust
Places to hide from the sun disappear altogether.

I Will Wait Still More

Can you hear the calling of the loon
from far away with that lonesome tone? –
foreboding and terrifying at the same time
in cries of a demanding lostness
seeking help or saving we cannot give.

I feel that could be me at the water's edge
making those forlorn sounds into the air
and waiting to hear responses telling me
I am not alone in this barren place
where I can see my reflection with the sky
comprehending the meaning of neither.

I want to hear the coming flapping of wings
bringing another to land on these waters –
I wait in my nest among the sticks at the shore
of this lake edge I like to claim as my own –
this lake I call in echoing hoots at three a.m.
for all to know of my existence on opposing shores
but for now I wish for companionship and comfort
I will call even more, hoping another will come
to lift my spirits from my fear of being abandoned.

Was It Sleep?

I woke up in my sleep

To complete emptiness

Of a bare space

In half-light

Complete silence

Even empty of air

Is it a place of beginning

Or one of final ending?

No sensory input

Except uncomfortable sight

How to describe

Nothing to see

Nothing to hear

The only feeling is fear

A terror of misplacement

Disorientation

My mind has never met this before

I hope to not meet it again

Desert Dream

He stumbled on a cactus

Fell on the sand

A young scorpion wagged its tail

Hottest sun burned his flesh

He stood and walked on

A life he remembered

Appeared in mirage

Decisions to be altered

Forgivenesses to be sought

Repentance to be believed

Blinding sunlight making him see

How they used to talk hours on end

About all of nothing important

How rides in the country excited

Like smiles and melding flesh

Before these things vanished

As did mirages on their own

He thirsted

For sanity

Not sure he wished to be found

Step after step

Sunk and bogged in sand

Muscles ached

Head spun

Destination forgotten

Only destiny remained

My Mother

Her longing for back when

Was palpable in her speech

Dreamy-eyed she would conjure

Images and sounds of long gone

Places peopled with common thoughts

Making butchers, delicatessens, cleaners,

Department stores, theaters,

radio programs live again.

It seemed like a foreign land.

We would listen to the stories and

Wish we could have seen and heard

Such things instead of Imagining them.

Her eyes were our eyes

Former happiness came alive

In times of playing

Laughing

Discovering

She was so much like us

Yet so very different

It helped us love her

All the more.

Come Dance With Us

Soon they said we could come on out
Like ballet dancers to twirl about in
Delicate pirouettes to rhythmic notes
Of heart enlivening love for our ears;

Where we were had no meaning to us,
Simply the joy of such freedom of expression
Pushed us to wide grins and smiles
Cool air brushed past our spinning faces;

Here is where the world turned correctly
We reached for each other's hands
Formed our slow churning cone of unity
Spreading exuberance to every open corner;

Take us home together in our glee
To where we know cherished memory
Of dancing the celebrations of happiness
In never-ending smooth vibrations of ourselves.

Dry Run

Someone crawled in through the window

Stealthily

as if on a mission

I heard them down the hall

yet the window was unopened

the sashes never slid

But I knew – I knew!

I waited for the footsteps

I listened for the door

Slight floor creak

Darkness surrounded like ice

Waiting met the silence

Imagination filled in no blanks

Sleep overcame awareness

Startled awake

I heard the outside door

open and close

and nothing more

Whomever it was

had left again

I felt quietly relieved

in my confusion

What had it wanted?

Why had it come here?

Just imagination?

I got up

Checked windows and doors

Locked

I pulled aside the curtain

Peered through the window

My breath streamed the glass

I found scrawled

"not yet"

What Does One Do While Waiting to Die?

The days of planning efforts to be made
For accomplishments or embellishments
In life of seemingly endless tomorrows
Vanishes in a haze of 'how did I get here?'

Death was always something that came
Somewhere else to someone else
We should have known better
Arrogance led us astray

There comes the constant question of 'why?'
As if a definitive answer would materialize –
An answer that would satisfy to let us
Relax into the unavoidable reality of physical being

Crying out brings empty solace
The mind refuses comprehension
Anger in frustration gains no goals
Friends run away for lack of words

Misery is something felt that needs no explanation
Pain rises in ways never before experienced

Tomorrow becomes the fear of worse and more
Night is another repetition in sleepless anxiety

Of what good is depression when faced with death?
How to define a vacant look at tomorrows?
Prayer feels as if it stalls in the air
Prevalence of desire holds the call to run in place

No one can truly help though their help is implored
Thoughts wander through a catalogue of 'what ifs'
Involuntary terror is its own device of distraction
Private tears flow in pleading to those not near

Memories rise and fall in their sense of meaninglessness
Yesterdays of years ago dangle their retention vividly
Reminding that most of those people are gone too
Opening doors to why would it be different for me?

An endless recycling of sameness lays itself down
The climbing along to be noticed subsides
An inevitable acceptance awaits in a near distance
For now tears fall on the fresh earth being dug.

What I Heard

We sat in chairs
Listened to stories
Laughed and drank more tea
Never knowing
What others had wished to be
Instead of what they had become
Still
Shared warmth in the telling
How life's road
In its twists and turns
Convoluted journeys
Bumped us as we scurried
Doing the best we could
Which never seemed like enough
Characters changed
Circumstances differed
Human wound up being human
We were the humor of ourselves
Happinesses and sadnesses
Were our indelible colors
Heard in the words we shared
Even In quiet pauses

We felt the air charged in reality

So

We sipped more tea

Smiled together

Settled back

To listen to ourselves

Being more alike

Than we could ever have imagined.

Does He Know?

When the sidewalks rolled up

I fell into the cracks

Nestled up in their strength and safety

For a good night's sleep

While inside I heard soft voices

Speaking freely not knowing I could hear

Does he know we follow his dreams to

Join with his emotional visions?

He knows without knowing

Our energy is non-threatening

Our faces are not memorable

Many times he feels our presence

Without caring who we are.

Rough concrete kept me sharp

Quick glimpses played themselves long

Everywhere was nowhere at all

Unfamiliar places seemed like I knew them

Purposes of actions remained unclear

Why was I doing anything in dreams?

Yet darkness of deep sleep finally satisfied

I fell comfortably into the realm of not knowing

No images or fears to bring to the surface

Birds twittered, sunshine slowly awoke,

The sidewalk relaxed its curl and I stepped out

Stretched and smiled with refreshment

Not very informative or entertaining

No, some nights are apparently just for rest

Oh, how boring

Better luck next time

They Sang for Me

I remember how a fading sun could bring sadness –

A sadness born of knowing happy times were ending,

Play was to be a thing left behind,

Excitement dimmed with the lowering light,

An unsettled feeling about what could possibly come,

A fear of the birth of twilight encounters never clearly seen;

I wanted to take a third breath I could not find,

A weight was on me to carry the coming of night;

Where were we going to go in the dark –

To places exuding a sensation of aloneness?

No matter the company I found myself in,

Security in love was not the plan for me;

Hollow were the sounds of owls calling

From high in the branches of thick bamboo,

Comfort came in the form of visualizing

Their stoic stance and certainty of place;

Robins sang through the night like nightingales;

I lie on my bed listening for far distant responses –

Concentrating on melodious distractions

Reminding me that beauty can be carried

    through the night on the delicate wings of song.

Nightmares Without Sleep

Too many voices speaking in pictures

Flashing as quick strobes behind closed lids

Like birds outside of an airplane window

As they blindly flock toward the engines

Too fast to be interpreted – just enough to feel crazy

Screams are needed to make the anxiety stop.

It's like a brain purge being watched as it hits

The subconscious in a sudden gushing leak

Causing no benefit to the shocked conscious mind

As it becomes inundated by the flowing sludge.

How to know behaviors of the brain

With neurons and synapses firing at their rapid rates

Following their own dictates (whatever they may be)

Having actions imposed on a helpless mind;

Why, where, who did what, flying by without reason

While leaving fear of unknown sources in their wake.

Run! Run! Escape from this maniacal spectacle assaulting

The confused senses in their vulnerability,

But yet when the storm has passed as quickly as it came,

No better sense of why can be gleaned any more than

Why did a tornado rip down every house in your block.

Angel Express

He held out his hand hoping something good would come

Perhaps from above or out of nowhere at all

Her hand reached out and gently clasped his

He smiled with closed eyes wanting nothing more

    Than the sweet feeling coursing through his soul

The great lands of plenty opened up far into the distance

His mind traveled the span in calm waves of shining breezes

Her presence guided them through fields of breathing life

Open freedoms called joyfully to his innocent self

    In senses surging forward to grasp everything at once

They settled onto the deck of a boat to the soothing sound of
    gulls

She laughed and touched his eyes to open toward the far shore

Trees glistened in pastel shades he had never seen before

The gulls took to fight and disappeared into the thick foliage

    When he too was suddenly on wings flying to settle in
        amongst the others

He heard her leaving without ever having seen her face

The gulls gathered on the branches around
    him to nestle close with warmth

Their united breathing brought his mind to peaceful serenity

His toes curled securely around the smooth wooden bark
His eyes closed themselves within the colorfully cool light
through the leaves.

Inside

People think we're not as pretty as frogs –

Them with their shiny iridescent greens and blues

And cute pinkish-beige underbellies against a window pane,

Gentle looking eyes of curiosity as they wait for bugs in
     the light

Or curl up in small contracted balls to sleep in safe crevices;

We, on the other hand, are toads – repulsive to most even
     in the saying,

Our skin has bumps and lumps in drab camouflage browns

And eyes that bulge in a dangerous looking way –

Nature gave us the ability to exude toxic fluid for our
     protection

But it has left us feeling much more abandoned than was
     intended

Jealousy is not our issue for we have our natural share of
     happiness –

The ability to run faster than frogs

The ability to successfully hide in the brush

We can wander much farther away from life-giving water

If only we could be viewed with the love we too hold inside

Wouldn't Together Be Divine

I write the words of how I feel
 I feel the words I write as well

In a whirlwind life beyond my choosing
 So many things to see and learn

I can spin as well as anyone else
 Becoming dizzy and disoriented at the same time

Tears are just the wet side of laughter
 From the inside of looking at yourself

There are cactus flowers side by side with daisies
 Beauty to be felt at sincere levels of our being

I hear blackbirds calling greetings from trees
 I look up to find them looking down on me

Ducks fly behind directions of their leader
 Heading for refreshing waters with safe places to hide

My smile is my own, born deep inside
 From knowing the value of good well beyond the bad

If you hear a snoring, it may be me
 Drifting along byways of unraveled dreams

You might even see the lines in my face disappear
    My breathing become soft and contented

If you hear your name being called
    It may well be me wanting you to join in

With what I can feel.

Memories in the Dawning Light

The sun starts to peek over the edge of the horizon

The sky reflects the freshness of glowing orange and pink

The blue of the sky brightens to its best azure tone

All in the silence of morning

I am delighted to be sitting by myself

Warming my hands on the sides of my coffee mug

Content to be filled with the same sunshine

In feelings emoted without compare

Memories of fresh dawn walks

Settling dew still to be felt in the air

My dog, Wolf, walking contentedly by my side

As we headed through the sleeping park

Amid live oaks and ducks lying by the lagoon's edge

We breathed in the quiet of streets

Celebrated the lack of shadows

Marveled at the freshness of it all

I sat on a rough concrete bench while

Wolf wandered to satisfy his need to sniff

When he returned, I petted his long dark fur

He sat relaxed at my feet

We stayed for long moments soaking in the serenity

The ducks slowly rose from their huddling,

Shook their feathers and did cursory preening

Before slipping into the water to find minnows of dawn.

We watched and then left for our satisfied walk back home;

As I sit here now, the magnanimous rising of the sun

Plays the same game of magic within my mind

As it did so many years ago –

A newness blossoming as if being carried in a basket

As a gift of incredible hope and fresh blessings;

I feel these things now as I drink my needed coffee

With Wolf by my side though he is long gone – yet

I can still smell the loved aroma of his fur

And feel his hair beneath my finger tips.

The Difference

I awoke to the thought that the day was Sunday,

I said "oh good, it's God's day",

But what met me was

An empty nakedness of a bare inside

An invaded space within my mind

I cried because God had left me

His presence could not be felt

It was like being left without a soul

I panicked for never having perceived such a thing

Everything had a complete feeling of nothing –

Nothing at all – devoid of every sort of realism

Absent of all that I had always known God to be

Angst on my part as to what could have happened

My mind was searching but not finding

Not like forgetfulness

I knew what I was looking for

It just wasn't there at all

Leaving me with the greatest sense of aloneness

I had ever known

Terror entered instantly like sudden unexpected mourning

I called out God's name again and again

I repeated " no, no, no" in my misery

Then I simply found He was there – inside of me once more

Just like all of my previous lifetime

I did not ask

Only accepted gratefully

It gave the definitive answer to

To the difference between

With

and

Without.

Here and Then Gone

On the beachfront

we listened to the wind

as waves rose

washed across the grass-studded sand

Wind brushed its effects

straight through our emotions

a sound like no other to our ears

Bringing excitement

Exhilaration

Curiosity

along with tinges of fear

carried on the unpredictable –

Mysteries inside of the wind

gave it personification

of simulated breathing

as if it could be a corporeal entity

plowing its way irreverently

uncaringly through our lives.

Then a softening would follow

in which names and voices

could almost be heard

in the inhalation toward a new start

before being swept away in a fresh surge;
There was a ferociousness in its howling
and whistling like the sound of extreme pain
Possible danger
being carried along as unseen secrets
yet the thrill of our fascination
continued
To follow the sounds and sensations
Believing we would be safe from harm
in the invigorating wind.
We were excited
by its passing across our skin,
the hair on our heads
trying to fly away in its wake
The force pushing against our bodies
to make us stumble
Then with amazing suddenness
the wind
stopped
as if a switch had been thrown
eerie silence ensued
It felt unfathomable –
where could it have gone?
We waited but the air remained still
As if nothing had just happened

Finally we shrugged

Thrills forgotten

And dove into the warm gulf waters.

Choices

Of all the gifts in the world to give

I would give to you

The gift of peace of mind

Would you receive it from love?

Would you let it envelope you

To take away your troubles –

Let all fears evaporate?

Bring an end to anxiety and terror?

Or would you rather stay

In your comfort zone of misery –

The known and familiar?

Which will it be?

Tonight

There is a sense of being left behind
Like not being picked for games in school
The need to smile when inside is broken
A period of aloneness that has no cure
Others may come without meaning
Not knowing what needs to be said
Afraid to reach out and actually touch
The wounded puppy lying in its bed
Tomorrow is always the question mark
Living in the land of maybe or maybe not
But for tonight I will hold on to the smiles –
The laughter I remember
The hugs and kisses filled with true love
Tonight I will remember who we once were

The Who Knows Conundrum

It's only when you die

Everyone discovers

It didn't matter that you were here at all

"You'll never be forgotten"

Lasts maybe a year

And then the forgetting starts

Azaleas bud and bloom in glory

Shine then shrivel and fall

The bush remains anonymous green

No thought left of its majestic blossoming

That is the way of nature

The repeating progression of life

Forget and move on the living say

I'm told the dead don't know anyway

We have no choice

We are ignorant of the truth behind it all

⠿⠿⠿

Chasing the Light

The spinning lights drove me forward

    I strove to find the source

Up, down, high, away – I tried to follow the stream

    You said I was wrong to chase such things –

Things that seemed to waste my time

    But I had different dreams than you

Collected visions of questioning the nonsensical

    To find the reasons behind accepted things

Lining the sidelines of dim grey emptiness

    My lights had colors that flicked switches

Effortlessly changing moods from desperation to smiles,

    From fear to endless love

From tears to laughter of the hysterical type

    I know I reached out to touch the light I chased

Birds ducked down to the blacktop to snatch up bread

    They flew away to heights I knew I could reach

If only I could catch the right beam of magical light

    The happy chase had guided my life

In so many ways you will never understand

    Even when it hid itself around a corner

Always did I know I could make a quick turn to find it again

    This light rolled and tumbled and jumped about

Through darkness of storms or in river beds rising
    Deep within caves of slow growing crystals
High up in the nests of nurturing eagles
    I ran with abandon, arms stretched wide to the sky
Free to be the epitome of a thirsting soul
    Satisfied in happiness to be invited to the quest
Then one day when my running slows
    My strength no longer what it was
I will wait anxiously for the day to come
    As my efforts are to be acknowledged
And the light will pause
    Then turn around
 To run toward me as its needed friend

Sergio

Sergio played the piano and sang to his heart's contentment
The sound was every bit for the soothing of his damaged soul
Notes both stabbing and caressing the air to drip with a story –
A story of pain and glory without expected harsh resentment,

He told of a private world put together with faulty glue
A father not coming home unless he really needed to
The sound of arguments and a grandmother who didn't
    interfere
A mother who loved without learning how to say "I love you",

Even when his head hung down again, Sergio played and
    sang on
The pain lived in his voice while his words drew pictures
    of what should have been
The music carried the heaviness of long protracted nights alone
While waiting for hidden goodnesses to crop up to be relied
    upon,

Prayers out an open window up to the quiet sky
He believed in the power of wishes along with the strength
    of love
He sank into the shell of himself not understanding who he
    might be –

Not knowing which direction to grow where could be found an
answer to why;

On he played, Sergio at the piano, singing words from times
long lost

Smiles and tears forming spontaneously to inner meanings only
he knew

Yet beauty erupted wildly as he brought forth the thick human
emotions

Yet most who heard him could never know what such beauty
had cost.

When I Fall Down

When I fall down will they come running

Or will I just be another tree in the forest?

Unseen. Unknown. Unheard. Uncared about.

Rains come and go like rare desert flowers

Reaching our minds just long enough to make an imprint

Simplified

I will write until I can't anymore

The words will only exist on what has been left behind

The vitality will reside within the lines

With no more to come

I will be the trunk in the woods

Lying on my side

Devoid

Of thought or

Creativity

A woodpecker will dive

Eyeing me

As his new-found friend.

ᔔᕄᕬ

What We Are

We run up the hill to sit on sun-warmed grass

The grand blue sky spread out around us

Grazing horses in the meadow valley below

Our smiles those of youthful discovery

Our being where we want

In the privacy of the whole open world

Hands touching, lips kissing, excitement building

Honey bees indulging in sweet clover

A repeated story for sure

Endless in needful recurrence

Who we are, defined in our laughter

Where we wish to go, shining in our eyes

Point to birds and shapes of white clouds

Watch horses nuzzling and chasing each other in play

We become a small piece of what we feel

Seeing is the knowing of our essence

High up on this hill, far above the mundane

Together we breathe in the truth of living

Thrill to the possibilities presented to our minds

Hold each other with certainty of belonging

Creating a bubble of combined oneness –

A oneness that can never repeat itself

For this moment is the only one that will come

This beauty is ultimate memory being formed

Food for our brains to feast upon

We could disappear together

Anytime

Just as specks

In the flaming nature of the sun

Smiling in the Face of Terror

I read the words you wrote to me. I even
Read in meanings that may or may not
Have been there. You say you are going to travel
To see how the world is put together. I
Applaud your enthusiasm and understand
The demand of curiosity. You wish for me to
Share joyfully in your mission. You wish
For me to forget about love. I have descriptions
Of where you will visit, places of fascination to
See, delicacies to be experienced, waters to be
Sampled and drifted upon. Concerts and operas,
Displays of modern and classical art, folk customs
And dances to clap for. All of these wonderful words
Fire the imagination to tears – my tears – as happiness
And grief combine to form
the most beautiful letter of good-bye I could
Ever have imagined.

So, How Are You?

I have lost myself

Gone forever

Not to be found

I am here

But not here at all

Sameness breeds frustration

Anger is now a companion

Friends have fled

(if they were ever really present)

Sanity is crispy

Crushed to dust

Love is a word

It still brings tears

Solo act of crying

No one even pretends to hear

Pain becomes irrelevant

Can anyone else know it?

Misery is its own entity

Excruciating is meaningless

Dreams

Fantasies

Processed thought collapsing

Question without answer-

How are you today?

Days of Ways

It's a quiet day on the sunny side of nowhere

Chipmunks forage for their seeds and worms

Methodically clawing the earth as silently as possible

Careful to not attract hungry predators from above

Then they scurry back to the borrow in the thick underbrush

To store the fresh food in a winter cache for later hibernation

Legs came slowly out of the huge green shell

Claws grabbed the moist ground to lift the heavy algae
    covered body

To pull it slowly free of the leaves under which it had
    been resting

He turned his head to look at me as the last dry leaves slid
    from his shell

Our eyes locked – thousands of years of evolution evaporated

We both knew he would still be here long after my passing

Still he let me know that hiding is often better than being seen

Ground and soil had better plans for him than they did for me

I had never seen the world as he had, just as he would

Not have wanted to have seen mine

He seemed to nod his head as he turned and started away

Around the hickory roots then down a ravine to disappear

Perhaps I would love to vanish into the long tunnels

Of darkness, safety, and contented solitude

Where the chipmunk has carved out its haven

Or maybe I could embrace the concept of travel

Within the adventures nature would freely present

While I rode the firm back of the turtle in search of food

Perhaps I could learn the lessons of hibernation

Or knowing how to trust the sliding into where I needed to go

It all seemed to revolve around living in so many ways

Without actually being noticed doing so

Questions

I held my breath as I watched

Someone's life pass me by

Five men came in the door

Headed to the blackboard to vote

Like points of fearful bullets

I felt them strike my unprepared torso

A sixth person stood to watch my reaction

Why had the days gotten shorter?

Why does fright smother us at night?

Questions fired at me in rapid succession

Do you have any idea of what you've done?

Where did you lose the ascending stairs?

How many days does it take to succeed?

Who left you adrift for us to find?

Tears rushed to my eyes while my chest

Squeezed me like a morning orange

There were so many answers I thought I would know

Yet blankness blocked my every thought

Their implications seemed too right –

Open ended without even a breath of air

I am there scurrying away from the sun

To seek coolness for my suffering soul

I fear I know the meaning of it all but am not ready to see

Then an errant thought enters –

Why have the songbirds fled?

Straight Forward

Nice and easy was the hop of the sparrow

Across a small patch of concrete covered in crumbs

Stop, look, peck and swallow while keeping an eye on me

My fascination wanted to reach out and touch

To know if the simplicity I was watching

Was actually simple at all

Our eyes met

His head turned slightly with curiosity

A communication passed through us

Before pecking up crumbs resumed

My whole life seemed focused on the sparrow

Imagination wanted to fly away with him

To duck under eves

Shimmy into private openings

To feel a nest of twigs

To bring shiny tidbits back as decoration

Smell the scents of home

Feel warmth of a mate and hatchlings

Both of us feeding the brood

Watching them fledge

Then prepare for another brood

She and I together forever

In our endless cycle of love
He looked at me one more time
Then the sparrow flitted away
Taking my heart home with him.

Don't Ask

Did you ever sense something bad was coming?

Trapped in a place you didn't want to be

Being carried along paths not of your choosing

Trying desperately to find an exit

Yet it remained out of grasp like trying to stomp on mercury?

She was five-years-old when she came and stood before me

Her dark blue dress with tiny yellow daisies seemed out of place

"You're going to look in the wrong direction if you don't hurry"

My mind slammed against a wall trying to know what was
       happening

The girl disappeared as I found myself in the rarely available
       Yellow cab

Cruising the streets of New York City until I stepped out to
       near-empty streets

My skin crawled as I searched the stoops for someone
       named Rory

When a man in black coat and black rimmed glasses suddenly
       came up behind me

"Follow me. Sassafras is cooking and the window is closing"

Up flight after flight after flight to an open door

A woman with red hair and wearing a blue dress from
       the forties

Turned from the pots on the stove and asked,

"Can you dance? No? Good because there will be no dancing
     here"

The walls warped and the sharp smell of liquor hit me from
     behind

   The mirrors of a dark club.

A hand touched mine and placed a key in my palm. "You came
     for me."

"She said you would." Her costume jewelry was gaudy and
     out of place.

Two men came at me with guns demanding to know where I
     left the girl.

I ran through doors, down unfamiliar alleys, across nameless
     streets

Until I reached my apartment and jumped inside to lock the
     door.

The little girl in the blue flowered dress was waiting where I
     last saw her.

"Did you get the key?" I nodded and handed it to her.

She pushed it into the wall and everything morphed into an
     auditorium

There was an oboe, my oboe, in my hands

The orchestra was tuning up on stage

"You passed the audition. Go on up and take your place"

"The orphans are waiting to hear you play."

What orphans? Why am I here, wherever here is?

"You'll figure that out one day. For now, just play"

Then she disappeared through the wall, taking the key with her
As the kettle drums sounded in customary dramatic fashion.

I Heard a Voice Singing

I heard a voice singing

From impossibly far away

In another time

Laugh if you will

At what this says of me

But my ears did not deceive

Nor did my mind misinterpret

The notes being sung were smooth

Melodic

Uplifting and captivating

A song from deep within the clouds

Beckoning

Inviting

Massaging my soul

I sat and leaned against the trunk of a tree

My eyes closed

My ears followed the lilt of melody

I knew the singing was for me

Though the actual words were unclear

I could feel their meaning

Directing my actions

Sleep took me

I floated in the air with the song

As my companion and protector

Ahead were mansions

Glowing in pure energy

The soft song continued

A figure approached across a lawn

And stopped gracefully in front of me

She smiled

Took my hand

Touched my cheek

Then twirled and danced away

I watched the retreat without remorse

I awoke under the tree

The distant voice of song

Began to fade among the clouds

I smiled with happiness in my heart

Arose and walked toward home

Think what you will of me

I saw and felt what I needed

From that soft voice singing

Just for me.

❦❧❨

Hope

The time of cherry blossoms has awakened to Spring

Huge abundant buds line the branches of trees in a row

Like parade floats preparing to bring pink petals to the heart –

Petals to be sprinkled in ecstatic joy of
   renewal from long winter's grey

Delicate flowers of undeniable Asian poetic lore

Glorious whites and tantalizing violet-pink blooms

As large as the opened palm of the hand

Dotted a landscape and spoke of soothing tranquility

Captivating to the eye and heart like words of a romantic play

Exploding into immense clusters nestled together
   in impossibly thick bouquets

Cherry blossoms make us smile

The aromas bring a soothing refreshment

The colors entrance our captive minds

While reminding us of an exciting new life

To be enjoyed and dreamt of while they are here

Before an eventual fading and falling away

Into the pit of joyous memory

And hope for a next generation

It's in the Contentment of Where You Want to Be

He had twist ties holding his shoes together

Ugly and colorful at the same time

Pigeons dropped down from the roof

He shared little bits of bread with them in the alley

They wanted the old Twinkie he unwrapped

But that was too precious for kind sharing

The day was gray with a slight chill running through the air

Late September it must be, at least that was what he thought

One eye was swollen with purple and blue rings

Young punks with nothing to do had done that last night

When they stole his hat with the $2.63 it took all day to collect

A gray beak and pink feet pulled at his pants leg for more food

He shook his head and said they were out of luck today

The opposite brick wall of empty windows and rusting steel

Mocked him as he dreaded another day if endless walking

The search for compassion and kindness amidst the sea of
    selfishness

The streets were his home for a very long time and he wasn't
    ashamed

He could find what he needed wherever he went

There was his world and the outside world colliding every once
in a while

His memories of where how and why no longer held meaning
or pain

Someone stopped and handed him a dollar as he walked toward
the mission house

A little warmth to go with coffee and biscuits uplifted his
spirits

Smiles a very distant memory of unused muscles with unclear
reasons

He pulled a coverless copy of best-loved poetry from his
threadbare coat pocket

Sal, a mission regular, drew up next to him and asked to be
read to,

He obliged

Here we are, far from home,

Waiting for a bus to take us back –

Back to a sweetness of warm breath

Kisses and soft beds for sleeping safe

Kitchen smells of baking bread

A dog wagging its happiness to see us

A woman to touch our cheek with affection

These are the things occupying our minds

While we waited for that bus to take us home.

Sal wiped his eyes and nodded his thanks and disappeared
    out the door

The paperback was slid back into the coat pocket

Another new day of possibilities awaited outside

He finished his coffee and scooped up biscuit crumbs

To bring back to the cooing pigeons of his alley home.

Waiting

Self-made portraits abounded in her mind
Wry smiles, sparkling eyes, flowing hair;
Did others in any way see her the same?
She heard twittering of a freshly awakened bird
Sounds of celebration for a new day
It was like her calling out to the world –
Except her world refused to answer
She sat and watched shadows
Creep across the wooden floor
Like finger paints moving before drying
Her mind wandered into discreet areas
Wondering where beauty she sought had escaped
No voices sought her by name
Were loneliness and emptiness the same?
The tea kettle began its slow growl to a whistle
She rose and poured the boiling water
Into her favorite paisley cup
Over a bag of aromatic black pekoe
To steep before bringing the cup back
To the faded sofa with her.
Would she make today one of melancholy
Or one of optimism?

Would her art shine or disappoint?

She knew her talent could flow and flood

As well as turn and swiftly drown

She breathed the steam

Took a slow soothing sip

And paused to listen again –

The twittering of her morning bird returned

But this time with a distant reply

She smiled

Maybe this time the world

Would give her the same.

Stairs

The staircase I climbed was that of love

The old wood creaked with every step

The varnish had turned dark brown

In its thick cracking and peeling designs

Worn down to sway-backed wooden planks

Willing to keep reaching up toward Heaven.

At the top I flung the door wide

Stepped out into an unknown space

The love had disappeared

I beat my fists against the sky,

Fell into a field of forgotten dreams,

Disappeared inside spinning whirlpools;

Taken under complete cover of darkness

Into spatial gasping of fading melodies,

I heard muffled echoes of a life never lived;

My legs longed to dance wildly to savage beats

Spiraling body movements of lost ecstasies

But paradise felt like false intermission

With floors ready to be ripped away.

Centuries passed without leaving a mark

A new mask fitted itself to my face

I suddenly had a smile I could feel

Eyes opened to a fresh rising sun

It was ready for us to sing the chorus

Voices joined in the secret refrain

Something had been found

Something had been avoided

The stairs took me back

To where I belonged

Collapsing forever into swirling dust

Behind my every step.

How It All Changes

The longer you live, the more you find out
That even related, you're nothing alike –
Quirks of personality instruct perception
Rocking chairs over loungers prove the point;
Forgetfulness is a natural pain reliever
Altering the past into a more palatable form
While pets with warmth and love
Retain their sharply imprinted motions;
I heard calls of loneliness and despair
Fears of being left alone
When a mind could no longer keep itself company
The blackness needed someone else's color;
Siblings cry for different reasons
No one can truly explain
Graves can feed the living with sadness
Others feel relief at the end game;
Corn is ripening on the stalks
Ninety days since Easter planting
Some can't remember what Easter means
But they always love sweet corn and butter;
When 'run around the corner' is an impossibility
And distant clarity becomes just a blur

Memory can lose facts out of time

But

I can always hear my mother calling my name.

Staggered Images

They ran to the edge of the clearing
Blue Jays squawked
Then quietly waited
The show was about to begin

Clay said to Carrie " are you ready? "
The forest ran deep
Hunters stayed away
Rabbits listened from hutches

"We gave up the world that didn't want us
We can learn as we go
Build what we need
Eat what we know"

"Sunrise for breakfast
Stars for protection
Canopies for shade
Moss for warmth"

Nods and smiles followed suit
Fears vanished
Excitement became life
New members for nature

Clay had knapsacks, Carrie had sleeping bags
Holding necessary planned survival
Teenage tears had driven them away
As surely as forced rejection and exile

A tiny stream ran through the northern quarter
Summer sun sparkled on the surface
Carrie sat on a rock and cast a string with hook down
Clay gathered wood to build a small fire

The bass was smoked on its bier of twigs
Silky stream water washed it down
Clay leaned back on one elbow
"do you have a name?"

Her hand reflexively touched her belly
"I think we should have a naming day at birth"
He nodded agreement
She leaned and kissed his lips

Bushes rustled
Squirrels ran up trees
Chased each other across branches
Then into their nest of young

Fresh clean unspoiled land and water
Bonded couples at home together

Normal return of necessary senses
Even if only for one divine day
of freedom.

What Will Become of Me

Live without knowing

When the last moment's coming

Feel the tension in the air

Time isn't slowing

For the quick torments' storming

Grip the life of a burning flare

Woke up this morning

    With a spark in my eye

My brain flashed lightning

    Just to see you next to me

I always wanted to be your dream

    I always needed to be your flame

Whatever will become of me

    When you don't look at me anymore?

⧉

Palms Against a Living Sky

In such tired arms I hold my head
   Tears no longer stream with sobs
      A cold rhythm plays in my brain
         Searching for the lonely island I lost
      Palms in motion against a living sky
   Water lapping its whispers somewhere nearby
Cool sand with sparse grass is against my back
   I don't have to look at the sun to know it's there
      The same with your eyes to know when I'm not
         Another time of asking how I got here
      Somehow there was a wrong turn made
   Even though I never realized I was moving
Now I hear seagulls calling as they seek the pier
   A pylon for safety and reprieve
      I could fish but no longer have the will
         I could swim but have no purpose
      Yet my soul wishes for peace of certainty
   While my heart remembers true love
I can see no future to plan for
   Nor a cessation of long emptiness
      As the whip-poor-will calls through the night
         Then goes home alone in the dawning light

The Coming Return of the Past

In a final time of a season's end
I have whispered into the breeze of October
I have sat to listen to the words of
    my one true love
Longing to hold hands once more
Before fleeing
    into the face of the moon;

Hear me calling out to you in the voice
    of a song,
Dance through the melodies of your mind
Lay your troubled head on my shoulder
Like many years ago when you needed
    this love that would never leave
Because you were more precious than
    you could know;

Our summer breezes brought us together
Your eyes brought forth poetry from my heart
I felt the mantra of 'she's my woman' burning
    in me
I strove for personal perfection I could never reach
Time strode on its perpetual conveyer belt of
    beginnings and endings;

Spring will eventually come again
For you to take the warmth of forever
    embraced
Into your heart to gallop over hills and
    glades once more
As you ever fill our one goblet with love and grace
Until comes the day, we will have to endure,
    when our Heaven must cry.

Confusion of Belief

What's all the raucous in the empty

Aisle of light? Did someone forget to close

The sacristy door? I am told there was

A tree involved but, then again, maybe not.

They did, however, drape themselves in flowing

Finery trimmed with heavy gold fringe and tassels

To carry monastery crosses of crude wood

Through the streets strewn with fresh cut flowers,

Believers and the pious with their hands clasped

Lined the old dirt roadways to pray with the

Passing procession. Religious holy days were

A highly sought celebration of God's graces for

The well-being of the small remote town. I heard

Her calling out with the voice of incessant misery

And pain, her voice cracking like ancient marble

Under the shifting weight of crumbling columns.

Her tears were those of genuine need and belief –

A seeking for relief through repentance of sincerity.

Those close by rolled their eyes wishing her to close

Her mouth and go away –

She was ruining their spiritual moment.

A Mother's Eyes

Looking to the left, looking to the right
I want to find another place to be born
Gentle hands to my face, soft kisses to my cheek
Deep love in a mother's eyes

Safety in the arms of she who won't let go
Tender words of attention and guidance
Help to raise me up beyond the clutches of fear
Pride in a mother's eyes

This is what I want, this is where I wish to be
Point the way so I can follow that path
A place waiting for my new arrival
A glory for a mother's eyes

In Days Past

Entrances to the park were closed for the night

Birdbaths and fountains still gurgling on their own

I could have felt helpless as I walked the fence line

Yet my legs still carried me faster than my heart liked

I leaned against the railing with hands grasping cold iron

While remembering past yearnings for slow solitude

Places where time seemed irrelevant amongst the trees

When natural formations surpassed those made with
    human hands

I wanted to be wandering paths by the accompaniment of
    birdsong

And droplets of sunlight sparkling their way through branches

Moments when expressions of true love reigned supreme and

The world itself seemed a very fine place to explore

It was times as those when incentives to be more than a worker

Gave off the alluring aroma of freshly gained creative urges

Yet now I mourned the presented opportunities I missed

The times I knew better than going back to following
    the crowd

My hands gripped the cold iron wishing the pall of night
    would lift

But the iron matched my broken heart harboring the scales
    in my eyes

Somewhere beyond I believed my aspirations still resided

In lush greenery along those paths I forgot to follow.

Running to Find

Sidewalks filled with crawling ants

Or were they people from an airplane view?

Cracks were forming where the apples fell

Like a new creation dropping dead on the ground

You can see them running

Hair flying in the breeze

Frost covered mountains waving greetings

The willing are on their way in droves

A handful of plenty is the purpose of searches

Look to the well of desire for drawing up dark secrets

Perhaps an empty bucket might not be a good thing

But a narcissist needs only a reflective surface

At the foot of the mountain the running dash stops

Cabins of greyed wood volunteer their protection for the night

Sunlit morning gives the stone its cap of gold

Upward is the beckoning of the communal climb

Will they find where the flies hide?

Engrained is the obsession with higher being better

Climb beyond whomever you may have been

Folklore is being written for generations to come

The mountain may well be a buried pyramid
Pointing to the grand star of destiny
A portal inside the brilliant cap of gold
Transporting all to the full seat of the mind

Rocks crumble and tumble under skillful grasping
Powerful legs and arms being the propellants
Finally a reason for the struggle of life
Finally a way to look down into the mouth of truth

Natural Drive

Cookies drew the grasshoppers closer to home

Green glory seemingly flying through the air

A funny hop down a street of desire

Awakens chivalry toward the admission of love

Where to fulfill the mating demands screaming

Long willful calling for beauteous sights unfolded

Nighttime flight for traversing past city steel

Finding leaves and stems and gobbling other insects

High toward the heavens where it is difficult for

    Humans to see or interfere

Empty city skyscrapers show the flashes of green

Streaking by plate glass windows until rest calls strong

Strong winds through cavernous valleys embraced by brick

Green, green, green by the hundreds

      swarming to songs of Spring

Buzzing of rapidly strengthening wings in furious flight

Escaping those wishing them harm or extinction

Away from stiff cruelties of steel and into luscious foliage

Offered in the park of darkness and abandonment

Shadowed within the safety of shadows on shadows

Succulent leaves and attractive blossoms

Bringing satiation to the great drive of hunger

Then the need for a mate ignited the hunting flame

To search earnestly for the most perfect procreation

Zigzag Escape

She ran moaning into the forest

To escape the onslaught of imminent foes,

Their pounding footsteps matching cadence

With her pounding heart in such a way

Like demons feasting on the faces of innocence;

Twigs and brambles recalled hurtful stings

Of a past long thought to have been forgotten

Snares whizzed by in hummingbird blurs

Skies crashed into crimson disasters

Raining down gray dust of abandoned graves;

Her tall ears swiveled frantically

Tuning into the sounds of homecoming guidance

Tiny almost imperceptible exhales exaggerated

Until she became a dart in the targeted hole

Lying darkly at the rooted foot of the ancient elm –

Just in time to hear double-barreled blasting reports

Of the dreaded wood and metal stick of fire

Warm furry ones behind her shivered

She sniffed the air but no burnt pellets struck the ground

Their warren remained a camouflaged invisibility

Relaxed shoulders let the bootfall crunches fade away;

She turned and nuzzled those huddled behind her

No more lurching away from those lain down on the leaves

Lost ones were to be remembered in dances of escape

Tonight would be for rolling in clover under a full moon.

$$\text{\huge Cups Held Separate}$$

I think I will write what I think

Only if thought is affordable

Blue-eyed dogs looked at me –

What else would they do with blue eyes?

Sunglasses might help but . . .

Across the street sat a beggar

Looking a great deal like me

When passing cars blew their horns

Their ire at his existence being plain

What were they expecting in response?

Litter rolled down the dirty street

Breezes tumbled wrappers acrobatically

Where did the tossers expect the refuse to go?

Secreted into thirsting holes in the ground?

Instead it all sat in soggy piles

Very much like neglected children everyone ignores

Not wishing to own their own creations

"This isn't my street" just isn't enough

Bad smelling people pass by

Thinking luxury must have a stench

It seems to be a learned trait of aging

My tongue hangs out from desire to gag

Names of those I don't know escape my lips

They lift their eyes from half-empty cups

I can't help what an errant brain triggers

Maybe they were yearning for someone to notice

Beyond the constant thrum of surroundings

Caring not at all about personal existence

So why should I be any different?

It certainly is not because I want someone to answer.

We are all stranded strangers

Wandering in an alien environment

Looking in a mirror doesn't help

I don't know who that is who is curious about me

Heads back down

We go back to our tasteless liquids in cups

Containing the empirical definition of separation

I stir the idle spoon to hear the scrape of sugar

Words flash in my paused mind

A dog shaking its wet fur from dripping rain

Sends chills through the emptiness

Of this hollow man.

How Did We Get Here?

It must be documented somewhere
The fall into captivity
Such a magnanimous event
Would never be ignored
Born to be scooped up
Trained to be a follower
In the great human herd

Passengers must be riding on something
Even if it can't be seen
The whole point of the exercise
Is discernment
Where am I being taken?
Who designed this tram?
Did I actually volunteer?

Golden flecks fall from the sky
I put my hand on the intended grave
Why do we have to visit dirt
When laughter is so much cleaner?
Precious things come out of the ground
We put dead things into it instead
I have trouble with this math

Stones and rocks and boulders

Hold fascination with forming under pressure

Judgment calls as to which to consider

Precious and which are to be cast aside as useless

Still the surface is covered with castaways

Filling our minds with awe

Upheaval of climbing features

Some stabbing the eye of the sky

As waves crash against rocky shores

In sprays of orange and white

Walk through an encrusted doorway

Step into a future past

Underground and overland

To reach a central core of control

Breathing its last breath of failure

For what has been created above

It's Okay to Look

Feel the upliftment of knowing who you are –
Live inside of your shell of incredible discovery
Only you know the hidden intimate spaces
Explore them all to your heart's content
Sometimes you sneak up on yourself
Guilty of ambushing waking dreams
Creative glee travels the same paths
Often choices need to be made
What you have seen and what you know
Are not always the same
Set personal alarms to know which is which
Reality fades in and out in different stages
Dependent upon where you wish to be
Personalities shift according to the recipient
Find who is living in those rooms in your head
Turn on the lights and let them come forth
But be prepared
They are not all going to be who you thought
You were,

Above and Beneath

The lonely traveling tide

made it to the shore

spent from its long wandering journey

Smooth is its stage of arrival

The moon takes a cooling dip inside

for under the surface

is the hidden realm

Jelly fish waver

as they bask in white moon spears

appearing and disappearing

with pulsating glows

Standing on wharves

lets you gaze down

into dark secrets with

mysterious tales to tell

Rainbow steps

put you beneath the surface

Unseen current

pulls you irresistibly away

Your own brand of tentacles

propel you forward

to dip beneath

dark arbors of coral

for seeing

who pokes their head out in curiosity

Vibrations of life and living

within the coral

comfort your soul

as you settle beneath

a particularly animated branch

of beige delight

Your supple body

blends into the color

You squirm gently

to be disguised in the sand

Night of hunting

in a luminous shade of green

was productive to a level of

Satisfaction

Changed now

to a mottled brown skin

The den of your home

let's you guard yourself

Under gathered rocks –

Sleep calls strong

within and without

your existence.

❧

Next Handful

Fingers pushed down into soft earth

Cool granulated pieces of nature felt joy

Sensory pads signaled the reality

Sent strange satisfaction to the brain

Not much different than ourselves

Feeling the relatives of creation

With their stories to tell of beginnings –

Events linked together in forges of fire

Bringing forth life in animated forms

See within apparent disguises of camouflage

That which lives beyond sight of the eyes

Heartbeats of the earth reside in simple dirt

Your touch to invigorate and be invigorated

Energy exchanges for continued existence

Feel it for yourself in your next handful of soil

Seekers

When love takes center stage
Other endeavors loss importance
Tunnel vision is the grand arbiter
Finding the differences between us
Wrong things demand in whys
Right things gain wily smiles
Not all is as it seems
Is it the way you look
Or the way you talk?
Lips have a lot to do with it
Eyes get their share
Hair has the importance too
Philosophy of dreams emerges
Past angst draws its pity
There is also the element of saving
Love – A grasping of being grasped
Sometimes a journey of desperation
Always the desirable necessity
To touch and be touched
Arouses
To love and be loved
Satisfies

Heart of the Rose

Sidewalk corners curled

I walked upside down

Like the turn of the century

I was about to become something else

New and refreshed

But the same

Crashing headlong into myself

Over and over again

World dangers walked away

I tumbled into a prestigious patch

Roses without thorns

On every side

Turned their delicate faces toward me

Speckled or solid colors of luxury

Royalty coming face to face

With me

Me with my unequal self

Strange lanky limbs

A ball with eyes on a stick

Being smiled upon

I stared into the abyss

Offered by the largest purple rose

Its golden stamen drawing me in
Caressing my different form
Then down, down down
Without trepidation or fear
Directly into its very heart
Within the soft petal embrace
Like motherhood swaddling her prize
Where childhood resides
Simple in its complexity
Wonder-seeking in its soul
Piercing my best shields
Probing my instabilities
While showing me the power
Residing in impermanence
The drive to get it right
The first time around
Those without eyes
See clearer
Love cleaner
Share freer
Intellect beyond my own
I fell asleep in great comfort
To be carefully expelled;

The sidewalk righted itself
I leaned momentarily against a wall
Where I had been closed my inner eye
Opened a deeper knowledge
Of how my steps should lead me
Without lurching uncertainty
Left in their wake.

Goats and Lambs

Pressure laid heavy against their thighs

A bleating lamb jumped for joy

Goats continued to graze

Captured sheep waited their turn

Marketing not in their vocabulary

A sweater of a thousand strands

Has no inclination to remember its origin

Washed away memories in bright dyes

Twisted into shapes never meant to be

Weavers have no care for what was stolen

Lives disregarded past the level of survival

Sheep followed goats through a mountain pass

Goats found a trail leading upward and departed

The sheep sounded their sorrow for inability to climb

A shepherd's voice reached perked ears

The gamboling home accompanied joy

Forgotten were the adventurous grass-seeking goats.

Lost Vision

A face of white lifted itself to look me in the eye

I could not see where the darkest tears fell

They were shed after all from my very eyes

I shake in the battlefields left before me

What blood – what blood flows from my veins?

Is there a predestined ending to the world?

I am the crispy one standing in the corner

Gingerly sipping an extremely hot latte

The faces disappear beneath the white foam on top

I must be swallowing those I don't know

My eyes hide in places unknown to my consciousness

I keep trying to see the completely unknowable

It is my face becoming featureless within its frame

Preparations for losing whomever I once was

For now the hot liquid must remain my friend of comfort

Before I traverse the battlefield of repetitions

Trying to face myself again.

What Exactly is Treasure?

Senses of treasure

Enticing through icy air

Pectoral flexing in anticipation

Eyes widening with glee

Turn to the mauve sphere

That's demanding her attention

Dragon scales held within

Tumbling in iridescent glory

Catch the eye

Mesmerizing

Hypnotic twists in a thirsting mind

Fires of questing ignited her craving:

She pondered what treasure could be hers

What offering to come undeserved

Left right up down – direction not apparent

She would know his eyes if she found them

A taxi arrived to take her away

Trepidation pounded her heart

Could this be the journey she sought?

"Where to, Miss?" (disinterest audible)

'Beyond this concrete and steel' was her desire

No answer seemed good enough

She decided on shops in the old part of town

Wind blew flurries of snow in small circles

She entered the store of older things

The smell of other lives filled the air

A scarf reminded her of her Nan

White leather gloves fit her nicely

She wandered over to old paperbacks

A tall man in a leather jacket was there

"Do you know if Rimbaud's poetry is good?"

He flashed the creased cover her way.

"Sorry but I'm not familiar with him but

I do love poetry"

"That's okay. What can I lose for a dollar?"

He had the eyes and the smile…

Maybe…

On the way to the register he introduced himself.

"There's a coffee house next door. Care to join me?"

Dragon scales tumbling

Flashed through her mind

Snow flurries outside

Hot coffee inside

Companionship and conversation

She agreed without thought

Her heart was in charge

Her hormones raced

Maybe…

Maybe…

Falling Skies

Cut out paper figures
Climb the mountain trail
Evergreens hide the marks

A taut bow string twangs
The arrow flies straight
To an unprotected heart

Blue skies collapse on cue
Deafening applause proceeds
From a fiery cracked earth

Bullets plead their case
Being not contrary
Mistreated innocent flowers

A pen to poke an eye
Knock knock
Everyone is here

Let's stroll the graveyard
Read the names aloud
Wait patiently for replies

A wind rips branches

The willow withdraws its roots

Is Mother Nature Listening?

Flipside of Daylight

The moon crept closer to my legs

Hoping for a deeper look inside

Nothing prepared could fulfill its requirements

I let the examination continue

Being draped in silvery white

Broke the spell into bits of a fresh recipe

New colors emerged from dripping silver

Forming rivulets destined for greatness

Can I feel the detachment

Of cold lunar rock around my ankles?

Flags have been planted in the bottom of my feet

I think the craters have found my face

We seem to be one

Pulling at each other's gravity

Even though solitary existence is cold

There's warmth in knowing your companion

If I ran out of the moonlight

Wrongness would descend

I couldn't abandon a friend

Burned Diamonds

Spears of destiny rose from pits of burned diamonds

Flew under their own power of perpetual motion

Skewering every entity they encountered without slowing

And circled the earth for centuries headed for a gathering

Of those who chose to feel the brilliance instead of the death

Left behind from the piercing of the spears.

'Awaken! Awaken!' Cry the bringers in long black dresses

Of maidens in mourning with lanterns held high

'Seek and see the ways held deepest in your mind'

'Find the self living behind the curtain of imitation'

'It is the other one you talk to when you are alone'

'It is the one with the power to save yourself if you wish it'

The spears are falling destitute to the infertile ground

Someone's time has expired where the clock no longer runs

The lanterns have been extinguished because
    the maidens married

Feeling good has become the temporary necessity of comfort

How empty shall the shell be of old age to come

Nothing more left but the scarred and blackened diamond
    that could have been.

In Days Past

Entrances to the park were closed for the night

Birdbaths and fountains still gurgling on their own

I could have felt helpless as I walked the fence line

Yet my legs still carried me faster than my heart liked

I leaned against the railing with hands grasping cold iron

While remembering past yearnings for slow solitude

Places where time seemed irrelevant amongst the trees

When natural formations surpassed those made with
    human hands

I wanted to be wandering paths by the accompaniment of
    birdsong

And droplets of sunlight sparkling their way through branches

Moments when expressions of true love reigned supreme and

The world itself seemed a very fine place to explore

It was times as those when incentives to be more than a worker

Gave off the alluring aroma of freshly gained creative urges

Yet now I mourned the presented opportunities I missed

The times I knew better than going back to following the crowd

My hands gripped the cold iron wishing the pall of night
    would lift

But the iron matched my broken heart harboring the scales
    in my eyes

Somewhere beyond I believed my aspirations still resided
In lush greenery along those paths I forgot to follow.

Rolling Midnights

Shadows were dark thoughts in the mind
Daggers of crimson flowing from my eyes

Confused brain bursts captivating thought
Trumpets sounding in howls of midnight air

I reach to grab notes of my life floating by
The smoky ash curls in disintegrating marble designs

Tapestries hung to folding colors on faded walls
Carefully crafted tales told in ancestral stitchery

Distant music of bygone times played mysteriously
I heard irresistible drawing powers slipping in time

Slow cooking brain reduced its voluminous size
Words fell carelessly from the mind brittle and dry

Another night of dark shadows swallowing my will
A midnight dream of forever rolling circles.

Remembering Nightbirde

She stood and sang with a light voice
Convincing in its nuances and meanings
It was a melody of original lyrics –
A story of her life trying to escape cancer
Her eyes showed contentment with her status
Her smiles and thoughts were those of positivity
She even stated "You don't have to wait until
　　life isn't hard anymore to be happy"
She only had a two percent chance of survival
And her response was "that's better than no percent.
I wish people understood that"
Her shining happiness and joy was stunning
Her singing was exactly what your ears could enjoy
Her attitude was beyond anything expected
It was uplifting in its display for us to drink in
For us to absorb that which she already felt
And knew
She died months later but left behind
Her reminders of perceptions and gratitudes
Being larger than just our petty self-pitying habits.

Reaching

I can no longer leave by the door

Legs are leathery heavy items of no joy

Dance steps are foreign memories

Perhaps they belonged to someone else's life

I have heard the voices out in the hall

Saying it's not enough of a story to be interesting

My escape is through lost windows of trauma

Remembered visions simmering like fish head soup

Pigeons on the ledge rest quietly next to me

Together we watch the air between buildings pass

There's nothing left that I wish to hold

Cooing comforts have a deeper meaning to me

Laughter still clings to my walls if I step inside

I feel the active motion of lost smiles

My angst is looking in the mirror

And finding no one there

Oblivion seems so very far away.

Bad Memory

I recall sitting next to those crying

Little ones lost or seemingly left behind

What can true tears be made of?

Suffering inside to pictures gone dark

Futures erased in the snapping of fingers

Answers as to why remain unavailable

His small hands were ready to learn crafting

His mind the bright mill of creation

Her mind sought the beauty in sound

Turning every direction to find musical expression

Giggles, smiles, clapping of happy hands

Fell silent in rooms of pillows and stuffed animals

One wet road – one mistake – one last hot scream

Solace is lacking, explanations hollow in falsehood

Small boxes lowered into an uncaring ground

I sat next to those crying

Too stunned for coherent thought

Voices in my mind to never be heard again

Actually See What You See

As you move through the world

Pass yourself in so many faces

Looking down or anticipating forward

There go more of you

Reaching for things

Stepping off curbs

Laughing with a friend

Carrying goodies home

Holding hands

Giving hugs

Heal yourself

Heal the world

Say hello to yourself

Everywhere

The Missing One

When dust settled on the wayside
The road became its quiet lonely self
We sat in shade thrown by the fig tree
Nibbled on freshly picked figs
Destinations a distant thought
Blue horizons and blue waters calling
Reasons to move slipped through our fingers
Past perfumes and flowers cast down
Sent waves across our idle minds
Someone we couldn't recall seemed missing
A voice not being heard increased silence
We glanced at each other with empty eyes
Looked at our hands and nibbled some more
A red-shouldered hawk called from overhead
It glided on with no moving prey in sight
We rose with our packs on our shoulders and
Moved onto the dirt road in mild sunshine
Hills ahead said that would be where we belonged
We felt amenable in our wandering need
The missing one seemed to be simple naked love
With a vibrant lily in hand
Perhaps it was what awaited us ahead
One foot followed another hoping this to be true

Castle Yore Reprise

Empty parapets next to naked windows
Listened to the low whistling of the wind
Nesting pigeons moved closer to discreet corners
Worn stones are curled against each other

Where had gone the arrows and the blades?
Who held the songs of coming victory?

Memories of baking bread lived in the walls
Children running up and down stone steps
Could be heard in the still air of the night
Weeping for lost loves echoed there too

Findings of our humanity left behind
We watch pieces of ourselves fall away

Ivy crawls hungrily up the shifting walls
Swallows build intricate nests in the eaves
Crows land on ledges and tilt their black heads
To eye the emptiness before swallowing a bug

Imagination cannot fill in human comings
Who decided everyone would move out?

Fountains

Fountains flow to their emotional rhythms
Cascading exactly how we wish for our minds
Content with splashes and choreographed pounding
In the air mist fanned out gracefully

Long breaths let us hear the plopping of water
Falling off trays of white marble and plaster
We remain enthralled with the skinny rivulets
And upward spraying flourishes of bubbly foam

It all seemed just as fascinated to be entertaining
Showing off its twist and turn acrobatics
Feeling our great smiles of admiration –
Our desires to share these magnanimous moments

Mysterious peacefulness pervades the soul
Our mesmerized attention increases
We become a type of oneness with the motion
We are visiting an inaccessible place in ourselves

Metamorphosis

I would much rather be playing in the sand

Than watching caterpillars devour succulent leaves

Hearing them crunch and drink the life away until

Nothing but a yellow-green stalk remains intact

Butterfly or moth to come

Metamorphosis a plain mystery

Tiny shortened lives in circles

Beauty as transient as rainbows

A wink – a blink and then there is no more

Yet colors and shapes remain fixed in the mind

After-images left imprinted on fortunate retinas

Freedoms inferred by fluttering delicate wings

Models of becoming confuse the stubborn brain

Tactile understandings motivate a material world

The great transformation seems too spiritual

I fear I had better simply stay with the sand

Another Return

In speaking with others roaming the platform
Answers were filled with impatience

Is this the right train to Hammersfield?
Where . . . Never heard of it. . . I think so . . .
You should probably ask somebody else . . .
Do you even know where you're going?
Silence. Scorn. Discomfort. Arrogance.
Impatience all the same.

Give up on the frivolous journey of curiosity
Back to sidewalks with shops with windows
Daydreaming about goods on display
Chess sets and handbags with gloves and jewelry
Seeing things of interest I never would have thought of
Walking and looking is dessert for the soul
Best sellers in a bookstore window
Reflections for a missing hoped for life
Watching or hearing interactions of others
Provides unusual entertainment
Temporary respite from a silence waiting at home
Parents rolling strollers with future greats inside
A tall man passes with a tiny fur ball of a dog in his arms

Where will the bicycles land after whizzing past?

The streets are dark with oil and burned rubber

Roaming people look very in private pursuits

Pho Lin is on the corner smiling his smile like everyday

Handing out discount tickets to his cousin's authentic
      restaurant

Perhaps a good meal would make the journey home pleasant

Sounds of dishes and mixed conversations with foreign accents

Aromas of cooking vegetables, chicken, even rice

Hot tea to steep while the mind roams over nothing special

Wishing to smile without anything to smile for

Paying with pleasantries without lasting meaning

A brisk walk toward home – the hours of wandering over

Hard to imagine these places and streets being empty

The curtain of night having the power to shut it all down

People gone like quick magical evaporation

Importance of purpose carried away into temporary oblivion

The front door opens and closes

Inner fading light is rather comforting

Desmerelda the tabby meows her welcome

And sits patiently by her dish near the counter.

Us or Them

Particles of nothing fall and cover us all

Coating our very lives with dark and light

Residues that pulse in alternating activations

Blinking on and off in random yet set ways

To direct things we do and don't do unconsciously

Touch – do not touch –where to find reality?

Liking or loving – where is the proof?

Seen and not seen move side by side

Sidewalks could be filled with those not there

Say excuse me to the phantom players you pass
    in the breeze

Hearing voices, music and singing, sensing presences

When and where no physical world proof exists

Turning to locate passing shadows that disappear

Listening to footsteps in an empty house

Black figures in corners and imaginary dogs barking

So, who is really here – us or them?

Both most likely.

Places of Questions

There are places in the world of the mind

Where my body has gone in life and dreams

Traversing landscapes and exploring buildings

Of tangible realities crying out for my participation

In motions of both realms;

Some people are voyeuristic, wanting to see blood

Other are too narcissistic to be interested

When I stood too close over the edge of a lake

Fear overwhelmed me as if I would uncontrollably fall

Drown – drown – drown – did that often enough already

Once in a pool, once in the womb, forever in the mind;

Tickle the rainbows I imagine could be forming

Over my head where I cannot view them

Sideways glance takes me into the trees

Where I flutter with groaning in the wind

Other side pulls me to the land of fantasy

Offering fabulous beaches in gleaming gold;

The sidewalk holds the words of a poet

Who spreads his messages to those who can hear

Sometimes soft in voice to create the building of beauty

Other times in loud vehemence to protest injustices

Some donate money for him to continue
Police threaten to arrest him for disturbing the peace
One way or another a hearing of truth occurs;

Clear waters of flowing fountains with coins tossed in
Promise that favors will be granted to the coins of begging
Hands and feet touch the cool refreshments
Idle minds disappear In the spray and falling waters
That clean the thoughts of deep weighted melancholy;

Even couples walking look lonely together
Far off glances the same as when they eat together
A union having disintegrated into uselessness of
Engrained habit giving animation to existence
Without desire to exchange even the smallest trivialities;

How to be worthy of being the one to be loved
Sparks cannot be allowed to abandon the fire
Sparse willpower withdraws to previous infertility
Tiredness of effort cannot be the excuse
A goal having been reached does not complete the game;

Agony over the fear of death in any aspect does not change
The next breath taken or none to be had
While we watch in disbelief as our worlds disappear
Under covers of just couldn't do it anymore
Or the demise of accumulated time alotted;

Where will I find the genuine touch of kindness?

When will be the brightest light of angst-free love?

I will breathe in the completeness of life

I will touch the beauty of soaring eagles

I will lie down in the arms of all that ever was.

When Is This?

Clocks can strike the wrong hours

Signal things rather not known

Theoretical of what time it must be

Having nothing to do with positional hands

When the words insist it must be time

When a life runs to its own end

When giving in is all that remains

It's an ending of one and beginning

    of another

Intangible by nature when passing unseen

Philosophical when nonlinear

Sadnesses thrive within encapsulated memories

Clocks cannot strike down the remorse

Wondering

Whenever things with wings turn to flight

I wonder where they go

As they disappear from my limited sight

Into places only the fliers themselves know

But what a wonder if I too could know

And feel their journeys, visit their homes

Know their lives as they know them –

Lifetimes so short yet filled with living

We discount them as trivialities below

Our need to know, beneath our existence

But who are we to conclude such things?

I would flitter with butterflies and moths

Buzz with bees and wasps

Hunt with flies and horse flies

Wing in the air with all manner of birds

See this same world with different eyes

Know different truths and values

Follow fresh instincts

Feel completely new emotions

If only I could join in

With their sets of celebrations.

☙❧

Another Fail

Where did Torrence Campbell go
dressed in his khakis, brown leather jacket
and cap?
It was three o'clock in the morning,
frost still clinging to the ground.
A cold dog barked in the background
white steam escaped with every exhale.
Was it purpose or panic in his step?
Sylvia Plaford, who couldn't sleep,
Watched through her dining room window
the quiet emptiness when she saw Torrence passing.
Where on earth could he be going at this time of night?
Her eyes followed him
insatiable darkness swallowed him like a ghost ship
passing in the night.
Torrence had never been the same
after returning from the war. They had known
each other since the days of school
even dated for a while
until his leaving for the service
ended it. He had never fathomed
how deep and total was her love for him.

When he returned nothing was rekindled.
They even passed each other
without speaking.
She turned her attention back inside,
folded a napkin next to the single placemat,
remembered her regrets at not trying harder
to touch his heart by offering compassion.
Even tonight
she could have signaled for Torrence
to come inside.
She sighed – another fail
Light suddenly flashed by her window.
A black vehicle was using a small searchlight
on the lawns and walkways.
Red taillights disappeared.
Unsettling
Sylvia headed back to bed
her mind still gripped with remorse.
Two days later
a brown leather jacket and cap
were found at the private airstrip
No log of flights from that night were found.
Sylvia knew more tears at night.

Unattainable

I reached for the sky

Believed I could grab a piece

Of what I could see

But couldn't touch

Reflected blues

Glowing whites

Puffs that make dreams

Birds crisscrossed vistas

Jets pierced clouds

Dropped contrails in passing

Ice crystals formed on my retinas

Secret hideaways

When I could have been

A gang of one

Looking up;

Up drains negativity

Like lilies dancing in a field

Knowing their allure

Somewhere inviting

Is the sky away from Earth

Away from pain and misery

Away from deterioration and death

Away from loneliness

Endless was the sky I seek

My heart needed it to be

I reached to touch

The unattainable

But I reach nonetheless

Bamboo

Innocence of looking through stalks of green bamboo

To gaze upon clear rain puddles reflecting blue skies

Mirror images of bright green leaves and vines

Topped with fallen yellow pollen floating at the surface

Tiny people travel through here on foot, on boats,

On wisps of wind to ride the green as we walk the ground

They fish under the fallen pollen to catch giant minnows

Run home under rain-dampened leaves

Then down beneath the earth where secrets are stored

Raindrops become great waterfalls of life

Vines with thorns are the barbed wire of safety

To have seen this through stalks of bamboo

Was the best of all my eyes and mind were capable.

Are You Listening?

Crying children, bleating lambs,
Signals of want from the forlorn
Who wish to be wrapped in robes of royalty
For your favors to find them worthy –
Worthy of love, hugs, kisses, security,
Companionship and high level unity,
To meld with you at the fibrous level of the soul
Conjoined to the rhythmic beating of your warm heart
Projecting the desire for exchange of fresh energies
For the needs of those calling to you for solace;

Hear with more than your crude ears of simplicity,
Feel with more than what you think you know
Exchange places with that which is calling to you
Because, in actuality, they both are really you,
Waiting on the help and attention of another,
Sensing there is more than aloneness;

Bleating lambs, crying children
You don't have to see to hear,
They live inside of your mind
Your brain recalls your own yearnings
How you felt needs without knowing why

How security kept drifting away
When a gentle touch suddenly brought certainty,
Turn that kindness on yourself
For the elusive trait of hope
To calm your anxieties and fears
To suppress unnecessary cravings
And let you become aware
Of responding to
The cries of the child
And the bleatings of the lamb.

Who Called a Halt

There is an impact from not knowing anymore
Not knowing the purpose of what you do
Not feeling the want to continue doing it
Losing the love for what you once held dear;

Friends are like railroad cars bumping and locking
Ready to pull each other one way or the other
Following and staying together mile after mile
Until we come uncoupled to wander away and lose touch;

Gains and loses lose their original relevance
We duck away from what we thought we wanted
Not knowing how these things could fade away
What can be called upon as important replacements?

There has been a numbness creeping past the gates
Filters in the mind are becoming non-functional
Roaming radical thoughts dart in and out of the emptiness
Even echoes of former selves has abated;

Like outer bands of rain approaching
We cannot prevent what is soon to come
Wishing for the drive of desire and ambition
To return brings no solace to a drying soul.

To Touch a Color

Eyes identify

Named colors you see

Elusive in tangibility

They are a trick of the mind

Being without reality

But known nonetheless

Residing in plain sight

You can touch a thing

But never the color itself

Blue soothes

Red angers

Yellow cautions

Violet uplifts

White purifies

Black mourns

To touch a color

Would be a never known

Tactile sensation

Beyond experience

O what would you be like

Great palette of known creation?

Where would my mind awaken

Swimming in a color of choice?

Follow the Flame

Fold your hands in silent meditation
Let your mind dig deeply into itself
Where to go in the swirling wilderness
Supposedly centering yourself somehow.
How to tether the untamable – the unpredictable –
The tender layers of who you have become?
A candle flame sizzles and waves gently for attention
You stare into its yellow, oranges, and reds
Imagining it as a lifeform dancing in place for you
Lifting you to a new level of awareness sparking life –
A life you have burning in the beating of your chest;

Flames and heat drive you with fascination
You become one with all that could be dangerous
But there is no danger in your journey through the fire
Your mind absorbs the cleansing dances of flames
You become the endless wick anchoring it to yourself –
The waxen image of what you were meant to be when
Formed of the simple elements of the earth
Filled with bursting passions and fiery desires
Buried within the tunnels of your docile mind;

Run with the wildlife that is your innate nature
Gallop proudly throughout the realm of inner peace

Pass all stale memories frozen from lack of resolve

Explore the cooling sensations of watery beginnings

Breathe the freshness of original awakenings

Sit beneath the trees of creation

At the foot of the sacred mountains of protection

Watch solitary wanderers on their own sojourns

Wait for the wavering flame to guide your feet forward

Rise to the rhythm of the timbre of your soul

Journey into the lost valleys of flowered peacefulness;

All of this ignited by the fire of the candle igniting your
      thoughts

Awakening you to a panorama of yourself in a light of glory

Making you shine with a revitalized light
      into which you were born

Placidly awaiting your entry into the meditation of existence

Where you are so much more than a lit candle on a candlestick.

Swaying Footbridge

I crossed the footbridge

Excitement thrumming in my chest

Flowing waters far below

Carved out rock faces on both sides

This was my way of flying

Safety in the rough ropes

Daylight between planks

A river gleaming its temptations

Wind swaying the bridge

Vertigo a thrill

Twenty people ahead of me

Twenty behind me

Where shall we go

If it all lets loose –

How fast the thrill

Of final endings

Long screams of escape

Experience like no other

I walk on

Hoping for safety

Longing for escape

Will leeks for the soup

Make it home?